Burdine's

Burdine's
SUNSHINE FASHIONS & THE FLORIDA STORE

SETH H. BRAMSON

Charleston   London

THE
History
PRESS

Published by The History Press
Charleston, SC 29403
www.historypress.net

All images are from the author's collection unless otherwise noted.

First published 2011

Manufactured in the United States

ISBN 978.1.60949.398.1

Bramson, Seth, 1944-
Burdine's : shopping in the sunshine / Seth Bramson.
p. cm.
ISBN 978-1-60949-398-1
1. Burdines (Department store)--History. 2. Department stores--Florida--History. I. Title.
HF5465.U64B873 2011
381'.141097593--dc23
2011038135

Notice: The information in this book is true and complete to the best of our knowledge. It is offered without guarantee on the part of the author or The History Press. The author and The History Press disclaim all liability in connection with the use of this book.

To the good and kind people, as most of them were, I worked with at Burdine's, primarily the employees of the food division of the downtown Miami store, and to finally be able to say "thank you" to them for the knowledge and insights they so graciously and unhesitatingly imparted to me, I warmly and with sincere gratitude dedicate this history of a once great company and its management, staff and customers.

Contents

Acknowledgements

To use the terminology of the latter Burdine's era, writing this wonderful book has been "a trip!" Whether reaching out to members of the community for input and material to include or digging into and through old files and archives, the journey has been nothing short of fascinating. One of my Florida International University students, David Batista, provided a number of Burdine's items for our use, while the Polk County (Florida) Historical Museum—through the kind assistance of Gail Seger, library assistant at the Polk County Historical and Genealogical Library—was kind enough to provide the society's June 1996 *Historical Quarterly*, in which the feature story was "Burdine & Son—The Bartow Store," written by the late John Burdine Crum and which provided a wealth of information on William Burdine, his store in Bartow and his 1898 move to Miami, which was meant to be a permanent move and not, as had been previously thought and written of, as a temporary move only for the purpose of establishing a branch of the Bartow store on the East Coast.

Don Boyd, who maintains a marvelous website of Greater Miami photos, came through like a champ—when I e-mailed him to ask him if he had any Burdine's images that we could use for the book, he did, but not just the usual suspects. Indeed, it was Don who provided the incredible—and very, very rare—images of the Burdine's store on Biscayne Boulevard in what came to be known as the Sears building; for his allowing us to use them, here's a special "tip of the Hatlo hat" to Don!

Longtime friends Andrea and Jonathan Nelson allowed me to use their 1951 Burdine's tearoom menu, and I am certainly grateful to them for their kindness in doing so. Miami Beach High graduate Roberta Small remembered her visits to the store, while Saralyn Nemser and her brother, Benjamin, shared their memories with me, as did their mother, Myrna Bramson. Barbara (Kaplan) Gertner took the time to, in her own inimitable fashion, bring her four years of employment at the store to life for me.

A warm thank-you is also due to our friends Anna ("Mickey") and Sherman Tobin, the former the first cousin of Burdine's longtime president, CEO and chairman, Alfred Daniels. It was Mickey and Sherman who, as Mr. Daniels's only Miami-area family members, saw to it that he was warmly welcomed, helped to arrange Westview Country Club membership for him and spent a great deal of time with him. Fortunately for posterity, they recorded much of his life's activities before and during his many years in Miami, remaining in touch after he left, ostensibly to retire but instead going to California to become chairman of I. Magnin's, the West Coast equivalent of Lord and Taylor or Henri Bendel.

Longtime (but not old!) friend Susan Carrey, a former neighbor, fellow Miami Beach High graduate and a twelve-year Burdine's associate, was just wonderful in offering help and furnishing information, and if the store were still in existence, a present from Burdine's would be the best thank-you I could offer her.

Our friends at the Fort Lauderdale Historical Society were most gracious in supplying information on the Burdine's store in that city, as well as on the municipal structures that it replaced. As they have been many times in the past, the research staff at HistoryMiami was completely available to share information with me on the family and the stores.

Linda Cicero, famed food writer for the *Miami Herald*, graciously shared several Burdine's dining room recipes with us, and while we were salivating, we were also thinking about how much we appreciated her help.

As always, a very warm thank-you must go to our IT director and webmaster, Adam Rogers, who worked his usual magic and relieved me of the worry of getting the images to our publisher in the proper format.

Regretfully, it must be noted that many of the Burdine's executives mentioned in the 1992 book that was written on the firm's history have now passed on, hence they are unavailable as contacts. Several of the executives who are still listed either in phone books or on whitepages.com did not return requests for information, and while Roddey Burdine Jr.'s phone in a western state has been disconnected, he did not return a request to his website for information and assistance.

Introduction

What a story! What an amazing and incredible story!

It is difficult to imagine, given the world-class city that Miami has become, that the entire region was, barely more than 115 years ago, a wilderness, replete with huge reptiles, hungry bears, panthers, innumerable snakes, rodents and other such varmints—as well as, perhaps, the most misery-creating of all, the mosquitoes. Oh the mosquitoes! Literally billions of them throughout the area, making life for the early settlers—particularly during the long, hot, humid, precipitation-filled and rain-drenched summers—miserable, if not perilous. And yet the idea of being pioneers, of coming to an American frontier in a place far south in a mostly unknown state called Florida, held a certain allure and attraction to a unique breed of men and women, not necessarily rough-and-tumble types (although there was no shortage of them) but rather people who saw opportunity and who would come to the southernmost part of what someday would be known as the Sunshine State to buy land, build homes, raise families, construct schools, open businesses and, most importantly, build a city.

The names of the first settlers, beginning in the mid- to late 1870s, from Gleason and Hunt to Sturtevant, Brickell, Tuttle, Collins, Pancoast, Merrick and Cohen, are well known to longtime Miamians, but the true and real beginning of what would, just a few years after it had become an incorporated municipality, become known as the "Magic City" is generally accepted as being the week of April 15 to April 22, 1896—on the former date the first

William M. Burdine, the founder, was a retired Confederate army officer, father of seven children by two wives, citrus grower, merchant and entrepreneur. It would be his 1898 trip from Bartow, in Polk County, Florida, east to Miami, in Dade County, that would set the stage for the birth, growth and development of what would, along with Rich's in Atlanta, become one of the most famous department store chains in the South, if not in the country.

train (a construction and supply train) of the fabled Florida East Coast Railway arrived on the shores of Biscayne Bay, while the first passenger train, carrying the legendary Henry M. Flagler, arrived on the latter date. It is from those two events that the commercial history of Miami emanated.

Brothers John and Everest Sewell long claimed that they owned and operated "Miami's first store," but whether there is complete truth to that statement is debatable, for it is also possible that the beloved Isidor Cohen, Miami's first permanent Jewish settler—having arrived at the Lemon City dock (at the time Miami's only usable ship-berthing facility) on February 6, 1896—may have opened Miami's first retail establishment. Interestingly, though, William Brickell was operating a trading post—which certainly could have been referred to as a store, since goods were bought and sold or, in some cases, traded to and fro—beginning in the late 1880s.

However, it would be the 1898 arrival in the fledgling city of one William M. Burdine (September 30, 1843–February 1, 1911) and his son, John M. (June 8, 1875–December 11, 1951), that would set the stage for the single greatest, and ultimately most famous, name in Miami's retail and dry goods merchandising history: Burdine's.

The Burdine's story actually began in Bartow, Florida, where William Burdine, with a partner, operated a dry goods store. When his partner left the business in 1897, Burdine was operating the store in Bartow when he heard about a dynamic frontier town on the far southeast coast of Florida; he moved there to open a store in the tiny, but already bustling, city of Miami, and the rest, as they say, is history.

Burdine's store grew through the early years of the twentieth century, thrived and prospered through the great Florida "boom" of the early to mid-1920s and successfully managed to wend its way, using careful and time-tested business practices, through the "bust" that followed the great "boom." Then, using the lessons learned in that time of declining business, and through the leadership of Roddey Burdine, William's son, it not only weathered the Great Depression of the 1930s but, no small degree, actually prospered.

With the coming of World War II, the stores thrived and business reached new heights. The 1950s brought Burdine's into national prominence, as much for its tag line "Sunshine Fashions" as for its later becoming "the Florida Store." The years that followed saw the company outhustle, outcompete and outlast all of its competitors.

The story not only of Burdine's growth but also of its importance to and impact on all of South Florida is inestimable, and whether being run by founder William, sons John and Roddey (October 14, 1886–February 15, 1936) or, later, by professional managers who were not part of the family, Burdine's would be a Miami (and South Florida) home-owned business until 1956, when, in a stock swap, the company, then with stores from Miami to West Palm Beach, became part of the Federated Department Stores holding company.

Under Federated's ownership, Burdine's would take over the equally famous Maas Brothers Department Stores on Florida's west coast, converting them to the Burdine's name; eventually, with stores in Orlando and other cities, Burdine's was a formidable statewide presence.

In May 2003, Federated announced that Burdine's would become part of its Macy's brand, and with that decision, a company whose name had been part of South Florida's business and, to many people, personal landscape and history for 107 years would fade forever from the Florida scene, leaving the Florida East Coast Railway (FEC) as the sole remaining corporate entity that has been a part of Miami since its founding—it is the one and only name and company with ties going back to the days and months before Miami's incorporation as a city in July 1896.

Coming to Miami

The story of how a great department store chain came to be is nothing short of fascinating, for it actually does not begin in Miami, which would be its home for all but the first two years of its existence. Instead, it starts in a small Florida phosphate-region town by the name of Bartow, in Polk County, which was named for a former American president.

The man who gave the Miami-based store (and, eventually, the chain of stores) its name was William Murrah Burdine, a retired Confederate army officer who, following that conflict, returned to his home in Mississippi, where he taught school and opened a drugstore in the town of Tupelo. His first wife died in 1880, leaving him with three small children—Edward L., John Marion and Estelle—about whom, with the exception of John Marion, we hear little. In 1882, he married Mary T. Freeman (July 15, 1855–June 9, 1929), and they had four children: Robert Freeman, Roddey Bell, William Murrah Jr. and Elizabeth, who would later be known by her nicknames of Bess or Bessie. For whatever reason, it is, for the most part, the "second" family, with the exception of John Marion, who appear prominently in Miami history throughout much of the Burdine's saga.

It appears that sometime in the mid- or late 1880s, the Burdine family moved to Bartow, where William Sr. felt certain that his fortune lay in the then very profitable citrus business. Unhappily for him—and the other growers in the area—the effects of the terrible freezes of December 1894 and January and February 1895 combined to change

"Beautiful, downtown Bartow." About forty-five miles due east of Tampa and roughly seventy-five miles southwest of Orlando, Bartow is about ninety-four miles west of Vero Beach, now a city on Florida's east coast. By 1896, Bartow was a southwest Florida crossroads, and it was a busy town even then. William M. Burdine moved his family to Bartow from Tupelo, Mississippi, in order to enter the citrus business. Following the 1894 and '95 freezes, which destroyed the fruit trees, Burdine in 1896 partnered with Henry Payne to open a dry goods store and trading post in Bartow. Although Payne left the business in 1897, Burdine, making a decent living for himself and his family, continued to operate the store. Although taken later than August 1898, when Burdine left Bartow permanently for Miami, this circa 1912–14 view looking east on Main Street in Bartow does show the exact location of the store, that being in the two-story building on the northeast corner of Main Street and Central Avenue, directly behind the large oak tree on the corner of the intersection of those two streets.

the fate of the family, as well as that of the place that would soon come to be named Miami.

Following efforts to replant beginning in mid-1895, William realized that the citrus business was not going to recover, at least in that section of the state, following the freezes. Enlisting the aid and assistance of Henry Payne, the two men formed a partnership and opened a dry goods store in Bartow under the name of Payne and Burdine, believing that, even without agriculture, the town had a future. It may have had, but Payne's association with Burdine was to be short-lived, and in 1897, for whatever reason, the two parted company, with Burdine maintaining the operation of the store and changing its name to Burdine & Son.

"Beautiful, downtown Miami." Coming to the tiny hamlet that would, on July 28, 1896, be incorporated as a city was nothing less than daunting, and the couple shown here, with all their worldly goods and a tent covered with palm fronds, must have wondered whether or not they had made the right choice venturing into the deep South Florida wilderness. Although somewhat improved by the time William Burdine arrived with his family in August 1898, scenes such as this were still in evidence just a few short blocks away from what was, even then, the downtown district.

Word, however, was drifting through the hinterlands of Florida of a wondrous new place on the state's lower east coast that had, on July 28, 1896, without ever having been a village or a town or an incorporated area of any kind, sprung into existence as a full-blown city. While not being told that Miami's streets were paved with gold, the reports filtering in and being carried by traders and transient merchants told of an incredible and exciting place, with a river named for the city that was so pristine and so pure that one could swim in it and the fish could be caught, cooked and eaten right out of the water.

Burdine felt that he would be doing his family a great disservice if he did not at least check it out, and with that decision made he left Mary and the children in Bartow, giving instructions to John Marion that he, as a member of the "first family," was to see to the management and operation of the store while William was examining this dynamic new place that had been founded by the legendary Henry M. Flagler.

Although it is not chronicled, and there are no known records of the trip in either direction, it is likely that sometime in late 1897 or very early 1898 Burdine boated around the southern end of the Florida peninsula and through the Florida Keys to reach Miami. If not this, he was possibly taken by guide across Florida, utilizing the primitive military trails, although he may also have boated across the state via one of the existing rivers, reaching the east coast, perhaps by using the Stuart or Jupiter inlets. In any case, he returned to Bartow completely enchanted. Several months later, as soon as John was ready to join him on the trek, the two headed for Miami to open a store.

When the first train of the Florida East Coast Railway arrived on the shores of Biscayne Bay on April 15, 1896, Miami had not yet been incorporated. A week later, the first passenger train arrived. The "Julia Tuttle sent Mr. Flagler some orange blossoms following the freezes, so he extended the railroad to the shores of Biscayne Bay" fable has been bandied about for too many years, and the fact is that no such event occurred. The entire story is a fairy tale that was concocted to lend romance to Miami's aura. In fact, it was debunked as early as 1913 by a promotional booklet published by the then incorporated village of Coconut Grove. However, by 1898, with the city having been incorporated two years earlier, there was an excitement to the place, a hustle and bustle far above and beyond anything Burdine had ever seen either in Mississippi or in Bartow.

Seminole Indians, thanks to William and Mary Brickell, who had been some of the Miami area's earliest permanent settlers and who had built a trading post on the south bank of the Miami River, were made to feel welcome beginning in the 1880s. The Brickells had arrived in the 1870s, and their names appear in the handwritten 1878 Revenue (tax) Collector's book, the oldest known piece of marked Dade County memorabilia in existence today, which is in the collection of the author. Along with black people—many of whom were from the Bahamas and some of whom were escaped or freed former slaves, transplanted southerners, carpetbaggers and scalawags (William Gleason and William Hunt were supposedly representative of that genre but, in reality, contributed a great deal to the east coast of Florida)—and other individuals from the Northeast and Midwest who simply wanted the opportunity to open a business and raise a family in an exciting frontier atmosphere, William and son John were caught up in the tumultuous activity. With the sense that they could be and

The Burdines—William and son John—had, just as William Brickell had, a ready-made market: members of the Seminole and Miccosukee Indian tribes, as well as the relatively small number of white and black residents. Shown here, in one of the earliest-known Miami photo postcards, is a mixed (in terms of clothing) group of Seminoles, the two women (squaws) wearing traditional garb, but the men, braves and children are wearing a variety of Indian and white clothing. The possibility of the suits on the men at far left and third from right having been purchased from W.M. Burdine & Son was quite likely.

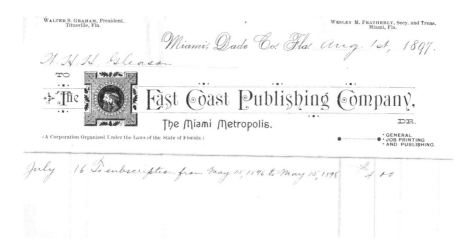

Truly, it was the frontier, yet on May 15, 1896, only one month after the first train arrived on the FEC and just a little more than two months before cityhood, the East Coast Publishing Company put out the first issue of Miami's first newspaper, the *Miami Metropolis*, of which only three copies are known to exist, one of them in the Bramson Archive. Equally important, though, is the fact that this might be the only known original *Metropolis* billhead, and this invoice, dated both July 16 and August 1, 1897, is for a subscription for two years, having begun with that first edition. The total for the two-year subscription was four dollars.

were going to be part of the growth of what all concerned felt would be a great city, they determined that Miami would be the ideal location for a "branch" of the Burdine store still headquartered in Bartow.

Julia Tuttle—who, along with the Brickells, gave Mr. Flagler half of her holdings (hers north of the Miami River, theirs south of the river) in exchange for his extending the FEC to what would become Miami and building one of his fine hotels—died of influenza in 1898, never living to see the city that she had helped create become one of the world's great metropolises. Though a pall was cast over the city with her death, recovery was rapid and the growth continued unabated.

Since a number of the illustrations in the first several chapters note addresses unfamiliar to readers and visitors who are aware today that Miami's

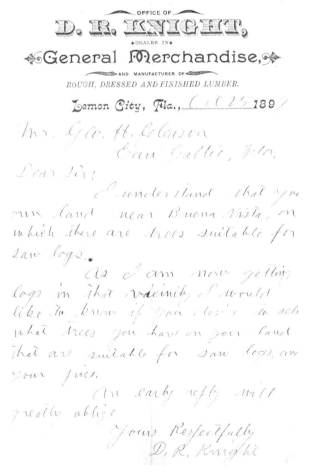

For several years, there was competition between Lemon City, several miles north of the area in which most businesses were opening, and what would become downtown Miami. One of the most successful of the Lemon City merchants was D.R. Knight—he opened his general merchandise and rough, dressed and finished lumber business several years before the Burdines made the decision to move their business to Miami. In October 1897, Knight sent this letter to George Gleason, who had moved to Eau Gallie, just north of Melbourne on Florida's east coast, asking Gleason if he would be willing to sell trees on his Buena Vista (a Miami suburb at the time, still in existence with the same name as a Miami neighborhood) property that Knight could use for saw logs.

streets and avenues are numbered using the quadrant system (northeast, northwest, southeast and southwest), it is important to explain that, until 1921, Miami's numbered streets began with First Street and progressed south in numerical order, with Twelfth Street being the main east–west business street. The avenues began with Avenue A, today's Northeast Third Avenue, and continued west in ascending order, with Avenue D becoming Miami Avenue in 1921, when the Chaille plan was inaugurated and the numbering and lettering system in place until that time was discarded. That avenue is today the city's east–west dividing street, just as Twelfth Street (which would become Flagler Street) divides north from south.

It was an incredible moment, not only for Burdine and his son but also for the friendly competitors who, in many ways—ranging from helpful advice to business references to assistance during difficult times—always seemed to be there for each other. The Burdines became friendly with, among others, John Sewell, E.B. Douglas, Frank Budge (who had the hardware emporium across the street from the Burdine store) and Miami's first permanent Jewish settler, the revered Isidor Cohen, who arrived on the shores of Biscayne Bay on February 6, 1896, and signed the city's charter, along with many of the other pioneers. The group was composed of unique and very special people who somehow managed to come together to shepherd the fledgling city toward growth and greatness. And William Burdine, who was there almost from the beginning, would live to see the beginnings of what eventually would be Miami's greatest retail dynasty and, indeed, one of America's most prominent names in retailing.

Burdine & Son, and Burdine & Quarterman

O n page four of her Burdine's history, author Roberta Morgan wrote that in 1898 William and John Burdine began what they thought was a "temporary branch" of their Bartow dry goods store in Miami; however, that statement does not actually appear to be the case. There is, happily, a record of exactly when Burdine closed the Bartow store permanently and moved to Miami.

While the 1992 company-authorized book *It's Better at Burdine's* offers no clue as to the exact date on which the supposed branch was to open (nor any clue as to how long it was to be a "temporary" branch), an article that appeared in the *Polk County Historical Quarterly*'s June 1996 edition, written by John Burdine Crum and titled "Burdine and Son—The Bartow Store," not only relates the complete story but also contains an ad that appeared in the *Bartow Courier-Informant* on July 30, 1898: "We expect to move our entire stock of goods to Miami next week." In that article, Crum revealed that Mrs. Burdine was having what today would be called a house or yard sale and was intent on selling the contents of their home in Bartow.

The *Miami Metropolis* on August 12, 1898, under the headline "Miami Is Fortunate," with a subhead reading "She Wins One of Bartow's Best Men as a Citizen," proffers the following to help to flesh out the story of the move, although it might create a bit more confusion:

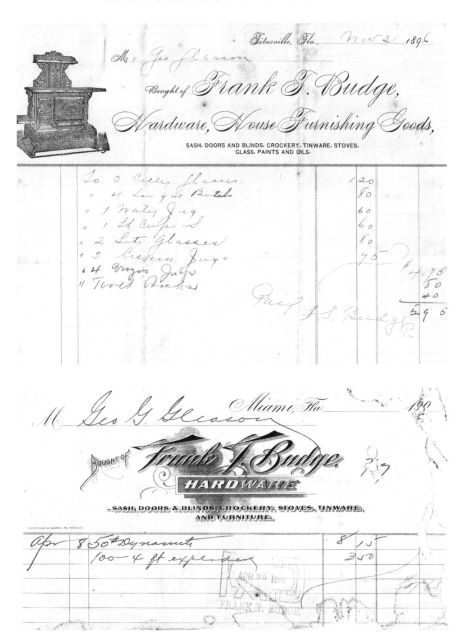

This page: Frank T. Budge, sensing the opportunity that the new city of Miami presented, apparently had the same feeling of faith and belief in what could happen there as William Burdine had. In 1898, Budge—who would occupy the building on the northwest corner of Twelfth Street and Avenue D, directly across from the Biscayne Hotel and catty-corner from the Burdine store when it moved to Twelfth Street—moved his business from Titusville, in Brevard County, on Florida's middle east coast about 210 miles north of Miami, to the booming new city. Shown here are two Budge Hardware invoices, an 1896 specimen from Titusville and a 1907 piece from the Miami store.

The Metropolis finds much pleasure in the announcement that Mr. W.M. Burdine, one of Bartow's best men and most valued citizens, is coming to reside permanently in Miami. The firm of W.M. Burdine and Son is one of the leading business houses in Bartow. A few weeks ago, this firm opened a branch establishment in Miami, with some degree of uncertainty as to whether the branch would be continued longer than the stay of the soldiers.

Under the management of the junior member of the firm, Mr. John M. Burdine, the business has proven such a success, and the attractions of Miami have been so great, that it has been decided to make the business permanent and the firm of W.M. Burdine and Son will be a fixture here in the future.

Mr. W.M. Burdine will move his family (and they are most excellent people) to Miami early next week. Their store is located in the Arcade row. Carpenters are now at work providing additional shelf space and one of

An original photograph of Frank Budge's hardware store, showing the northwest corner of Twelfth Street and Avenue D, with the store apparently preparing for either a grand reopening or a holiday celebration in July 1900.

the largest stores of dry goods, clothing and gents' furnishings brought to Miami is being opened up and put into place.
We are pleased to welcome Mr. Burdine and his family to Miami.

Sons John Marion and Edward, according to Burdine family legend, hauled the store's goods across the state by horse-drawn wagon in late July 1898, following the routes of the old army trails cut through the wilderness of Florida during the second and third Seminole Wars. Then, on August 3, 1898, William, with Mary and the children at his side and accompanied by Eva Quarterman, who worked for Burdine in Bartow, left their home and headed for a new life, a new store and, unbeknownst to them at the time, the beginning of a new chapter in the history of Miami.

When William and John opened Wm. Burdine & Son in Miami in August 1898, the city had a population of less than 1,200. Beginning the operation

Just as William's sons would take over the Burdine's business, so Frank Budge's son, Harry, assisted by wife, Gussie, would do the same for his father. Harry and Gussie, possibly in a rare moment of relaxation in a city abuzz with a great boom that was increasing business almost daily, are shown in another original family photograph, this taken of them on the famous palm walk at the Flagler System–owned Royal Palm Hotel.

with what John thought would be a very sufficient $300 in capital, the first store was housed in a 1,250-square-foot building at Avenue D and Twelfth Street (now Miami Avenue and Flagler Street), and it appears that the exact location was actually on Twelfth Street east of Avenue D.

While no photographs of that first store seem to exist, there are drawings of the exterior of it, and unquestionably, the store resembled a frontier trading post, being constructed of rough-hewn wood and apparently being twenty-five feet across the front by fifty feet deep. The store offered a limited selection of shoes, clothing, fabrics and sewing notions, lace curtains, table linens and umbrellas.

But why, exactly, did Burdine open the store? Why in Miami, and why at that propitious moment in time? One of the most apparent reasons was the Spanish-American War. Unlike Tampa, which was the main billeting and jumping-off point for Havana, Miami still managed to attract the attention of the army, which sent an estimated seven thousand troops to be trained and quartered in the city.

After having survived a Christmas morning 1896 fire that began on Avenue D south of Twelfth Street at or near Fourteenth Street and essentially burned the entirely wooden business district to the ground, Miami began to recover almost immediately, and by the time William Burdine arrived in 1898, the city was in the midst of a near boom as the rebuilding and extending of the city in all directions was well underway.

Interestingly, though, while many other recorders of Miami's history wrote briefly of that fire, Isidor Cohen, in his 1925 self-published *Historical Sketches and Sidelights of Miami, Florida*, mentioned the conflagration in no small detail. In his first chapter, Cohen wrote about the business community, the opportunities and the city in general, noting that in the "[l]ast part of December, 1896…Miami looks like a real town." Cohen wrote that "[a] t about one o'clock Christmas morning, shortly after the merchants closed their stores, flames were seen issuing from the roof of the building occupied by E.L. Brady, at the corner of Avenue D and 14th Street."

Cohen noted that all of the wooden buildings were destroyed and stated that "[t]he only remaining buildings were a two-story brick-veneer structure at the northwest corner of Avenue D and 13th Street, a three-story solid brick building at the northwest corner of 12th Street and Avenue D and a two story brick-veneer across the street from the latter." He also remarked that

It was a locomotive just like this one—a 4-4-0 American Standard type—that led the first passenger train into Miami on April 22, 1896, and though larger engines had been purchased by the FEC, a good few of these locomotives were still in FEC passenger and freight service in the early years of the twentieth century.

the only person killed was a fellow merchant, J.M. Frank, who was struck by fragments that had been blown into the air by "an exploding cylinder."

Once the Burdines arrived in Miami and were able to open the store, business began to boom almost immediately. Besides residents and some visitors to the city, the store catered to many of the local construction workers, railroad employees and soldiers, who it seemed had more leisure time then they did drill or field maneuver time and, for the era, seemed to be paid quite well.

In addition to the white and black customers, the Burdines were very comfortable catering to members of the Miccosukee and Seminole tribes and were more than willing to sell to them and trade goods. Bessie Burdine Read, in an article in the *Miami News*, remembered that "[t]he Indians seemed to like my father's store. He made them welcome as they would come into the store in single file and then shop in single file, one following the other in looking at goods and paying for their purchases."

Friendly competition was the order of the day in early Miami, and the Burdines seemed to fit right in. The Henry Flagler–built Royal Palm Hotel drew a high-class winter crowd, and that brought additional business to the stores located only a couple of blocks from the hotel and easily accessible

The famous Seminole Indian and Burdine's customer Tiger Charlie was a Miami fixture in the city's early years. Although outwardly gruff, he was a kind soul and became a well known and warmly welcomed Burdine's regular.

by horse-drawn hack or by walking, which many visitors did in the winter season when the hotel was open. Although William Brickell's trading post on the south side of the Miami River did attract some business, soon after the city's founding it became quite evident that business would center in what someday would be called "downtown Miami."

Among the merchants the Burdine boys became friendly with were Cohen, John and Everest (Ev) Sewell, E.B. Douglas (his estate, at today's Northeast Second Avenue and Fifty-second Street, would be sold years later as Douglas Gardens to the then Miami Jewish Home and Hospital for the Aged to serve as its new campus), jeweler H.T. Whaler, hardware entrepreneur Frank T. Budge (who had moved his business from Titusville, Florida, in 1898) and bicycle and motorcycle dealer J.W. Harper. Though a bit of a distance north, lumber and general merchandise dealer D.R. Knight—whose store was an anchor in Lemon City, several miles north of the Twelfth Street and Avenue D nexus of the fledgling city—also became a friend and confidant of the Burdine brothers.

Cohen, no longer operating a retail store but rather involved in other businesses in Miami and on Miami Beach, wrote the following in his 1925 book in regard to Miami's merchant class:

The material condition of a town's merchants is its prosperity barometer. This aphorism is particularly applicable to Miami. Miami's prosperity is easily discernible by an inspection of its leading mercantile establishments, particularly the highly developed four oldest establishments—W.M. Burdine's Sons, E.B. Douglas, John Sewell & Brother and F.T. Budge Company—and the two younger ones, namely Burdine & Quarterman Company and the New York Department Store. Every one of these prominent stores had a most humble beginning; their growth is symbolic of the general growth of the city that made their remarkable progress and success possible.

The reader will note the mention of Burdine & Quarterman Company, the genesis of which is as fascinating as the origin of the "parent" company. As with so much of the early part of the Burdine story, wherein some of the history is extensive, a seemingly equal amount is both elusive and difficult to ferret out. At this more than one-hundred-year vantage point of the past, sometimes it is difficult to put together, hence some speculation must be made, particularly in dealing with the departure of John Marion from W.M. Burdine & Son.

Roberta Morgan's *It's Better at Burdine's*, although written with the support of the company and published in 1992, is not only riddled with errors but also does not flesh out many of the details regarding incidents that are germane to the Burdine's story, leaving the reader wondering what happened and what the rest of the story is. The Burdine & Quarterman situation is a perfect example.

Cohen noted that, at the time his book was written and published (1925), Burdine & Quarterman was still in existence. And Morgan did note the beginning of the firm, telling the reader that "[a]s Miami grew so did the family's fortunes. John Marion married Pauline Quarterman, daughter of the store's seamstress (Eva) and he and his mother-in-law left the parent organization to open a ladies ready-to-wear store on the corner of Northeast First Avenue and Flagler Street." The problem, though, among others, is that no date was given in the Morgan book for that event, and what is stated as "Northeast First Avenue and Flagler Street" did not exist at the time when John M. and Pauline opened their store, the correct letters and numbers being Avenue C and Twelfth Street.

The other very valid question, of course, is why. Why exactly did John Marion leave his father to form his own firm? Conjecture might tell us that

This page: In their earliest years, neither W.M. Burdine & Son nor Burdine & Quarterman carried fine jewelry, leaving that to other merchants. In April and May 1904, William J. Krome, assistant construction engineer for the Florida East Coast Railway, came into Miami in preparation for the ordering of goods and material needed to begin construction of "the greatest railroad story every told," the Florida East Coast Railway's Key West Extension, which actually started on the FEC's Miami docks later that year. On April 14, Krome purchased an alarm clock from Whaler's Jewelry Store at 314 Twelfth Street (between Avenue C and Avenue D on the south side of Twelfth Street) and then, on May 13, purchased oil cloth, spools and needles for the outlandish sum of $1.05 from Burdine & Quarterman. This, made out to Mr. Krome, may just be the only known Burdine & Quarterman billhead, letterhead or invoice that exists in private hands.

it was either because he was not getting along with his brothers from his father's second family, or possibly because, as a new husband and with a talented mother-in-law who had been schooled in the business by his father, he simply wanted to make a name for himself and not be the "& Son" of W.M. Burdine & Son.

Fortunately for posterity, the Bramson Archive contains the only known existing Burdine & Quarterman letterhead, and that invoice, dated May 13, 1904, and shown in this chapter, notes that the Burdine & Quarterman firm at 308 Twelfth Street, having issued the voucher shown as its number 10628, had to have been in business for several years.

Morgan, following her misstating the avenue number and street name for the location of the first Burdine & Quarterman store, then proceeds to relate how William and John M. chose the location near the corner of Twelfth Street and Avenue D for *their* store in 1900. Hence, the best that today's researcher can hope to do, unless one can access Miami City Directories of the era, is to recognize that Burdine & Quarterman most likely came into existence some time after 1900. Given the number of the invoice shown, it is apparent that, several years before 1904, John M. and his father probably parted company, at least in the business sense, most likely in 1901 or early 1902.

Burdine & Quarterman, just as did all other Miami families and businesses, suffered the effects of the various hurricanes that to some degree brutalized parts (or all) of the city. For example, the *Miami Daily Metropolis* of October 19, 1906, noted that "the roofs of the Sewell, Burdine & Quarterman and other business blocks along 12th Street and Avenue D were damaged and the contents affected by the rain even after the wind had subsided."

Burdine & Quarterman had its own building, likely at the address mentioned previously. In a report on Miami's Huntington Building prepared by the city's Historic Preservation Planner, Sarah Eaton, in 1983 for the purpose of having that building declared a historic landmark, Ms. Eaton noted that the Huntington Building was developed by Frederick Rand. After discussing his background, Ms. Eaton noted that among his buildings that were still standing at the time of the report was "the old Burdine and Quarterman's Department Store."

William M. Sr. died on February 1, 1911, leaving his business, still named W.M. Burdine & Son, to his four sons: John Marion, Robert Freeman (May 15, 1884–1929), William Murrah Jr. and Roddey Bell, who was named

Miami's first permanent Jewish settler, Isidor Cohen, was a good friend to William, John, Roddey and Roddey's other brothers. Cohen opened his first store shortly after his arrival on the shores of Biscayne Bay in February 1896. A signer of the Miami city charter, Cohen, with Roddey and several other of Miami's early merchants, would found the organization that would eventually become the Miami (later the Greater Miami) Chamber of Commerce.

president of the store. William Jr. was appointed vice-president, while Freeman (Robert used the first initial of his first name, rather than "Robert," preferring to be referred to as "Freeman") became secretary/treasurer. John, though named in the will along with his brothers as a full partner, was at the time of William Sr.'s death still actively engaged in his own store, Burdine & Quarterman, hence his name does not appear as being appointed an officer in the business in which he was a partner with his father.

While competition in early Miami was intense, with such as the Sewell brothers, Isidor Cohen, the Lummus Brothers, E.B. Douglas, Frank Budge and others vying for the attention of the shoppers, there was no question that William Burdine Sr. was not only sharp as a tack but was also an innovator at a world-class level.

Burdine, it was reported in the *Miami Metropolis* of August 21, 1908, had come up with the idea (perhaps not the first time offered in the United States, but certainly a Miami first) of offering to pay the cost of out-of-town visitors' train tickets if they spent a given amount of money in his store:

Mr. Burdine has started a popular innovation, in that he will pay the railroad fare of any and all persons, one way from nearby places [how "nearby" was not specified], who buy $25 worth of goods and the fare both ways of persons who buy $40 worth. This is an inducement that cannot well be overlooked.

Not only this, but Mr. Burdine is giving to each purchaser a ticket, which is punched according to the amount of the purchase, and when the ticket shows the purchase of $15 worth of goods the holder is given an order for an enlarged photograph of him or herself, or any person desired.

The article went on to note that "Mr. Burdine's ad, giving more complete details of his bargains and the special offers that he is making available, will appear in the *Metropolis* tomorrow afternoon."

William had taught his sons well, and following his death and Roddey's ascension to the presidency of the firm, the company was incorporated and the name changed to W.M. Burdine's Sons, Inc. It was only logical that Roddey would become president of the firm—since graduation from Miami High School in 1908, he had worked at his father's side, learning the business as he did everything from sweeping floors and emptying trash bins to doing inventory and serving as a salesperson.

Freeman, who was two years older than Roddey, became a highly respected attorney in Miami, while William Jr., though interested in the financial aspect of the store, preferred the outdoor life. Spending a great deal of time in pursuits related to fishing and hunting, he eventually became friends with a good few members of the Seminole tribe of Florida, going so far as to learn their language. When the Indians would come out of the Everglades to shop in Miami, W.M. Burdine's Sons was the destination of choice, for "Willie," as he became known, would make them feel totally comfortable and quite often act as translator between customers and clerks.

John Jr., although involved with his own store, was consulted frequently, for he had been at his father's side in the business from their first day, and he remained close to his brothers. In any case, though, it was and would be Roddey who would initiate the growth of what would become a dynasty and lead the Burdine name to greatness.

A Growing City and a Growing Store

The city of Miami and W.M. Burdine & Son (and later as W.M. Burdine's Sons, Inc.) matured together during the early 1900s, the store's product line enlarging and expanding as the city did the same. By 1912, the store had evolved into a full-scale department store, with all of the modern merchandise and high-quality goods that were available in large northern and midwestern cities. Stores that had been quite successful in Key West, then Florida's largest city, were finding that it was becoming extremely difficult to compete with those upstarts in Miami.

With the opening of the Florida East Coast Railway's extension to Key West, and the moving of the Miami passenger station from Sixth Street between Avenue B and the Boulevard to its new location between Tenth and Twelfth Streets on Avenue E (later, 200 Northwest First Avenue), the Burdine's emporium was only a short walk from the depot. Many of the arrivals would stop at the store en route to their hotels, mostly the Flagler-built Royal Palm on the Miami River or the Biscayne Hotel on Twelfth Street but in some cases at the Peacock Inn in Coconut Grove, along with several other early-in-the-century Miami caravansaries.

Miami was beginning to be perceived as a luxury resort destination for those who favored the already-famous Flagler System hotels—particularly the three in St. Augustine, the Ormond in Ormond and the two in Palm

Roddey, growing up in Miami, had an enormous number of friends and was well liked more for his kindness and warmth than for his name, which, to his friends, mattered not at all. He was "Roddey," and that's how they knew him from youth until his much too early passing in 1936 at the age of forty-nine. This picture, which has appeared in print only once before, is one of the most incredible Miami photos ever taken. It came from R.E. Coates, who is shown seated between Freeman and Roddey, who was good enough to send it from Fort Meade in 1948 after he had moved there and opened a business. In this picture are some of Miami's greatest pioneer names. From left to right, posing languorously on the steps of the Royal Palm Hotel, are Dexter Douglas, Dave Tuten, Monroe Padgett, Gus Haseltine, Fonnie Talbert, T.N. Gautier, John Gardner, Roddey, R.E. Coates and Freeman Burdine.

Beach—and with the city beginning to be thought of as having a perfect climate (at least in the winter, sans humidity and blessedly almost mosquito free), the store began to reinvent itself to meet the needs of a new and seemingly more affluent and sophisticated clientele.

Roddey, who with the title of president had actually become the general manager of the store, began to reshape W.M. Burdine's Sons into a more fashion-savvy and style-conscious destination. In retrospect, with the beginnings of what that awareness would mean, the store would, some years later, completely assume an identity that reflected the subtropical location that William Sr. had been fortunate enough to have come upon.

Although the "Sunshine Fashions" slogan was not copyrighted until 1929, it appears that Roddey may have first used the term as early as 1914, which was the year he started to display the various clothing styles, colors and fabrics that were appropriate to Miami's delightfully pleasant winter climate, as well as the casual (at least compared to the formality of resorts farther north on the Florida east and west coasts) resort "feel" that Miami was beginning to exude. The store began to stock and show high-quality New York and European designer clothing, and in 1914, along with the "Sunshine Fashions" moniker, Roddey originated fashion shows in Miami, a selling tool that may have been a hallmark of such high-end northern stores as Marshall Field & Company in Chicago, Hudson's in Detroit, Hutzler's in Baltimore, Macy's and Gimbels in New York and other department stores in other major cities but was a concept new to Miami.

The quality of its clothing and other merchandise, as well as absolutely excellent customer service, became a hallmark of the store. Roddey, even at that early point in the store's history, introduced sales training and awarded bonuses for not only the generation of sales beyond what was projected but also for those employees who were the recipients of favorable customer compliments. Burdine & Son became the largest volume retailer south of Washington, D.C., and east of New Orleans, surpassing the largest of the Atlanta stores and earning Roddey Burdine the moniker of "Merchant Prince of Miami," carried proudly until he died in 1936.

But it was not just Burdine's that was growing. The increasing population of what would by the mid- to late 1920s become a world-renowned resort and the largest city in the Sunshine State was having an effect on a burgeoning metropolitan area and its environs.

There have been no few books written about Miami, from Victor Rainbolt's 1921–22 *The Town that Climate Built* and John Sewell's then contemporary *Memoirs and History of Miami, Florida* to Isidor Cohen's fine tome, referenced previously, and Tracy Hollingsworth's 1936 *History of Dade County, Florida*, which strangely enough has nary a mention of Burdine, either the members of the family or the store with that name, and further to this writer's series of sixteen books on the villages, towns, cities, counties and people of the South Florida Gold Coast, including *Miami: The Magic City*, published in 2006. In each of them, the sense of growth and greatness is entwined throughout the story. To understand the growth of Burdine's, one must also recognize and understand the growth of the city that was, for so many years, its home.

While this book is not meant to be a history of Miami, an understanding of the city and its growth will certainly assist the reader in comprehending

Among the entertainments for early Miami visitors, a trip up the Miami River, often aboard the excursion boat *Sallie*, was a marvelous way to see the deep and forbidding Everglades, and if one were lucky, on the trip out to or back from Musa Isle or Coppinger's, one would see alligators. Of course, one could always take the trip that led them to the Sallie Tower, and from there the explorer could see way out across the Everglades. Years later, this would become Northwest Seventeenth Avenue.

what that growth meant to and did for not only Burdine's but also for most if not almost all of the business establishments and service providers that had decided to either open a branch or to make Miami the home base.

There were settlers in the area beginning as early as the 1850s. Henry and Charles Lum landed their sailboat on a mangrove sandbar island that would someday be called "Miami Beach" in 1870. The Sturtevants and the Brickells were residents by the late 1870s. The "Commodore," Ralph Munroe, had first visited Coconut Grove in 1877. Despite all of this, very little would occur in terms of the commercial history of Miami until Henry Flagler signed a contract with William and Mary Brickell and Julia Tuttle agreeing to accept substantial amounts of land from them in exchange for extending his railroad to the shores of Biscayne Bay and, at the same time, building one of his great hotels.

John Sewell, who would later gain local fame as a pioneer and early merchant, arrived in Miami in late 1895 to oversee the construction of the Royal Palm Hotel for Mr. Flagler. The Royal Palm, for many years the largest, most fashionable and most desirable hotel destination in Miami, was the hotel that would, from the time of its December 31, 1896 opening until its ravaging by the 1926 hurricane, be the center of Miami's social, political and business life, frequented by residents and visitors alike and recognized today as one of the major anchors of an early and growing city.

In 1906, the first electric streetcar began operating, and though it would only last until 1909 (there was not yet the population needed to support a trolley line), full electric railway service was restarted on January 7, 1922, following a short-lived attempt to operate a streetcar system powered by huge storage batteries under the floor of each car. Eventually, the electric car lines brought passengers, including customers and store patrons, to downtown Miami over three separate systems operated by the City of Miami, Carl Fisher's Miami Beach Electric Company and Coral Gables Rapid Transit Company. The latter was built by the founder of that city, George Merrick, and had two separate lines running from "the Gables" into downtown Miami, including a local line that ran via Ponce de Leon Boulevard and Flagler Street and made all stops, taking about an hour and five minutes to make the trip, as well as a high-speed interurban line that ran on an all-but-deserted Coral Way at speeds of up to seventy miles per hour.

The Miami story, from its unlikely beginning in 1896 through the current era, is unmatched by any other place in America and is more suited to a fairy tale than it is to reality. Miami grew unceasingly from the moment of the arrival of the first train on April 15, 1896 (followed by the first passenger train one week later), as the trickle of humanity became a deluge if not a torrent.

On November 10, 1910, the U.S. Department of Commerce and Labor/Bureau of the Census issued its "Advance Bulletin of Population." Florida had between 1900 and 1910 gained 223,000 residents, its population at the end of the first decade of the twentieth century being slightly more than 751,000 people. The population of Dade County, with Miami as its county seat and by far largest, and only, incorporated city at that time (Homestead was incorporated in 1913, becoming the county's second incorporated municipality), had jumped from 861 in 1890 (the county at that time included all of today's Martin, Palm Beach and Broward Counties) to 4,955 in 1900 and an incredible 11,933 residents by 1910 (Palm Beach became a separate county in 1909). It more than doubled its size in ten years. Still not one of Florida's largest counties—there were twenty-three counties in

Florida with a greater population—by 1920, Dade would be fourth largest; during the decade of the 1920s, it would surpass all other Florida counties in population as it continues to do today.

Roddey and his brothers, because of their father's foresightedness and willingness to pioneer, were well positioned to move forward and grow with Miami. By 1914, with the First World War just beginning in Europe, that growth was about to explode.

The city, the state and the country saw that war come and go, and for a very short time following it, there was a lull in business, but by 1920, the population and the pulse of business was increasing daily. New people meant new stores and new businesses, and while the black community grew larger in Overtown and the Jewish community became more civically active, opening more businesses, offices and synagogues, people of every color and faith began the process of making Miami the melting pot it remains today.

With the coming of the Roaring Twenties and national recognition through the promotional efforts of first the Florida East Coast Railway and then the various land developers—including, among others, Carl Fisher, George Merrick, Merle Tebbetts, Ellen Spears Harris, Hugh Anderson and Harvey Baker Graves—the excitement here was palpable and the hottest commodity available was land; the young men and women who were the salespeople and who were known collectively as "the binder boys" were turning over parcels of land eight to twelve times in one day. Flagler Street, from the FEC tracks all the way east to Biscayne Boulevard, as well as other downtown streets and avenues, became a jumble of yelling, screaming young people attempting to interest passersby in buying land. Subdivisions sprang up in all directions, and the Everglades was relentlessly pushed farther and farther to the west. Roddey, with a heightened sense of awareness of what the future could bring, was poised to take advantage of what would come to be known as "the great Florida boom of the 1920s."

Roddey Burdine was a visionary, far ahead of his time both in the store management sense and in the vein of how to treat his employees. In his 1925 book, Isidor Cohen expressed his reverence for the man who was coming to be known as the "Merchant Prince":

Of Miami's pioneer boys, who stand out as examples to the youth of this section of the country, none is more eminently qualified for an honorable

A view from the west looking east gives a clearer perspective of the relationship of the hotel to the Burdine's store, which is to the east of it. The turret of the Halcyon Hotel, two blocks to the east, is visible on the left side of the street, while a row of pine trees extends from Avenue B (Northeast Second Avenue) to Boulevard.

place in the history of Miami than R.B. [Roddey] Burdine, whose success as a merchant is only exceeded by his achievement as a financier… Upon graduation from Miami High School the youngster entered his father's establishment and quickly mastered the business of dry-goods merchant. Upon the demise of his generally lamented father, he took charge of the store for the benefit of the surviving family. In 1912, at the age of twenty-four, he consummated the remarkable undertaking of the construction and stocking of what was then the biggest building south of Jacksonville, the Burdine Building on 12th Street between Avenues C and D. Within a few years Burdine's Sons business had expanded to an extent that an annex was required to house the greatly enlarged department store, which, under Roddey Burdine's direction, has attained its prominent position in the mercantile world.

Cohen went on to wax rhapsodic over what Roddey had done, and he noted that at the time he wrote his book, the Burdine building was five stories high and was often referred to as "Miami's first skyscraper"; it extended through the block from what by then was named Flagler Street (the former

Twelfth Street) to Southeast First Street (the former Thirteenth Street) with a frontage of 50 feet on Flagler Street, 250 feet on First Street and 240 Street on Miami Avenue, with a combined floor space that at the time aggregated 151,000 square feet.

The store, Cohen related, was a colossal structure that housed a modern emporium comparing favorably in magnitude and variety of departments with those of the most notable of the important cities of the country. The store, he wrote, "added materially to the prestige of Miami in its important contribution to making this city the shopping center of innumerable towns and agricultural communities within an extensive and rapidly expanding territory."

Roddey, who demanded that all of his employees be treated with respect and with appreciation for their work, was well ahead of his time in offering both benefits and bonuses to those who came to work for him, and many employees, just as with the FEC Railway and with Mitchell Wolfson and Wometco Enterprises, remained with Burdine's for decades. With Roddey's unending contributions to both his employees and to the good of the community he loved, the question might be asked today, "Where is he now that we need him?"

When Roddey built his five-story skyscraper, the city was in awe, for that building was the first in Miami with an elevator and the first in the city to be built with steel beams. With Miami at that time an ongoing and seemingly never-ending work in progress, and with air-conditioning not yet on the horizon, the constant construction in the streets and on neighboring buildings created an almost endless stream of dust, which kept the employees on the move, constantly wiping the merchandise and dusting surfaces to ensure that the store and its merchandise always appeared clean and fresh. In the meantime, even though the top three floors of the new building were at first used for offices, the store not yet having expanded to have enough merchandise to cover all five floors, business began to increase at an astounding pace, and new merchandise and new employees were brought in on an almost daily basis.

The various developers were doing anything and everything that they could to publicize the city that was becoming more famous every day, and with construction booming throughout the county and Flagler Street so jammed with people that police officers had to be stationed on every block to direct both the automobile and pedestrian traffic, it was at that precise moment that Roddey moved forward with another of his "outrageous" ideas (following his inauguration in 1919 of bonuses for the staff): the initiation of an in-house employee magazine, first called the *Enthusiast*, and then, starting in May 1926, the *Burdynamo*, which, for the first several years at least, appears to have been published on a monthly basis.

It was during the first years of growth following his father's death that Roddey recognized the need for additional trained staff. In 1913, George Whitten, following graduation from Stetson University and after having worked for Roddey for several summers, was hired full time. His first real job? To learn the business, and that was what George Whitten did as he worked his way from the stockroom to, eventually, the president's office, becoming the first non-family member to achieve that position. Although his career at Burdine's was interrupted by World War I, he continued, upon his return, to move up the corporate ladder. In 1943, thirty years after going to work for Roddey on a full-time basis and after years as vice-president and general manager, he became the company president, a position he held until 1957, when he moved to the position of chairman of the board, the company by then having stores from West Palm Beach to Miami, as well as on Miami Beach. In 1988, after having retired from the company in 1961, he passed away at the Villa Maria Nursing Home in North Miami.

Those years, from 1911 into the boom of the 1920s, brought great fortune to Burdine's. Names that resound in Miami history, along with Whitten's, who were part of the Burdine's story include Freeland Bland Cresap, Hiram Blakeley, Charles Crawford, Charles M. Hargrove, Rowland D. Saunders, May Lutrelle, Adelaide Lawrence (the store's first personnel director, hired in 1924) and the inimitable Madam Donan, who seemed to have no first name other than "Madam" and who was referred to by that deferential term even by Burdine and Whitten.

Madam Donan's story is typical of how Roddey would hire a person and then let that person "run with the ball" to create another success for the company. She was brought in as the buyer for the inexpensive dress and ready-to-wear department, which at the time was marginal at best in terms of either volume or profit. Upon taking over as the buyer, she used illustrations of elegant models, with the pictures becoming immediately recognizable in Burdine's advertising. The women in the drawings, according to Roberta

Morgan, were shown with "long hair, long skirts and wasp waists which got their shapes from 'ironsides' corsets." Madam Donan took charge of the department, which in 1913 had been allotted only a very small space, and in fourteen years, she had built the department to a size and stature of such importance that it occupied the entire third floor of the store.

In 1915, Roddey married Zada Dutton and brought her from Deland to be part of the family. They had two daughters, Zada and Patricia, and his happiness shone on his face as he walked around the store. It was a spectacularly good time, even though it was still several years before the great boom.

Eventually, the offices on the top two floors of the five-story building were emptied of tenants, and the store expanded its product line and its offerings. In addition to that expansion, Roddey arranged for the purchase of the two-story Chaille Department Store, which was located on the corner of Avenue D and Thirteenth Street and backed up to the Burdine's building. It was relatively simple to break through the wall and allow customer traffic to flow through the expanded store.

Much went on in Miami during those years. Whether it was the towering Seminole Indian Tiger Charlie purchasing an entire bolt of fabric for $108 from the tiny (four feet, eight inches at her full height) May Lutrelle, which was the largest single sale the store had ever made up to that time, or Captain Charlie Thompson landing a thirty-thousand-pound, forty-five-foot-long whale shark after a thirty-nine-hour battle and then displaying it on Twelfth Street right next to Burdine's, there was no end to the funny, sad, heartbreaking, loving, ironic and incredible stories that came from Miami's single greatest retail name, including the marriage of Bess Burdine to U.S. Navy lieutenant commander Albert S. "Putty" Read.

Read and Bess met at the Hippodrome Theater, which was located east from the store on Flagler Street. They were introduced by a mutual friend, and it was love at almost first sight. Married in a beautiful ceremony in January 1918, Bess would have two children with "Putty," and the marriage would last a lifetime, but he would gain worldwide fame when in 1919 he became, with a copilot, the first person to fly the Atlantic, the feat accomplished in a navy NC-4 seaplane.

The Reads were so warmly thought of that Helen Muir—discussing World War I activities in Miami in her book *Miami, U.S.A.*—noted that

43

[w]ith the influx of servicemen Miami matrons turned themselves inside out to provide a sample of Southern hospitality. Home entertaining reached a new high, romances flourished, and among the marriages that followed World War I meetings "down among the sheltering palms" were Dr. Thomas W. Hutson [Dr. Hutson is still active today and is a member and past president of the Miami Pioneers] *and Dr. Jackson's daughter Ethel* [Dr. Jackson was Miami's pioneer physician, and it is for him that Miami's Jackson Memorial Hospital is named; his former home on South Bayshore Drive is now the headquarters of Dade Heritage Trust, the organization that has done so much to preserve historic Miami and Miami-Dade County buildings], *as well as Bess Burdine and Albert Cushing Read, not yet an admiral* [Read's promotion to admiral was a good few years in the future].

Like her brothers, Bess never forgot her hometown, and after "Putty's" retirement as a rear admiral, they spent a great deal of time in Miami. Following his death in 1967, she returned to the city to live and spent her remaining years active in innumerable civic organizations, charities and philanthropies.

With business increasing almost daily, Burdine & Son in 1925 added a new six-story 150,000-square-foot building on Southeast First Street next to its original location. Sales in 1925 increased by 204 percent over the previous year, and a fleet of company-owned trucks was making deliveries to Miami Beach, Lemon City and Coconut Grove. George Whitten was appointed vice-president and general manager, and B.H. "Hiram" Blakey, who would later manage the Miami Beach store, was named men's clothing buyer. It was a very exciting time, both for Miami and for Burdine's.

The company attained a reputation throughout the northeast and the Midwest as the most fashionable place on either coast of Florida in which to shop or even dine. The company advertised itself in national magazines (the first and smallest regional department store in America to do so), with ads urging customers to travel with an empty steamer trunk so that they could fill it with merchandise available only at Burdine & Son. Because the store offered warm-weather clothing all year long, the Miami store proved to be an excellent test market for manufacturers' lines of spring and summer clothing before their deliveries to department stores in northern states. On no few occasions, store buyers going to shows in New York would run into people from northern stores who would tell them how clerks were telling the salespeople that they had already seen those clothes (or styles or fashions) at Burdine & Son (and later at Burdine's).

The boom was at its height, and in 1925, the brothers agreed that not only should they offer stock in the firm to the public but also, in addition, that it was time to simplify the store's name. In that year, in conjunction with the stock offering, the name of both the corporation and the store was changed to Burdines Inc. (However, the name on the store and merchandise continued to be "Burdine's.")

Proceeds from the stock offering were used to fund expansion and for working capital; because of the boom, another seventy thousand square feet of retail space were added to the Miami store.

With the name change, with business booming, with Miami Beach becoming a world-class resort and with Miami turning into a major business center, Burdine and Whitten were looking across Biscayne Bay, for it was there, they believed, that a new business opportunity awaited. Because of Roddey's friendship with N.B.T. "Newt" Roney, that belief would soon be proven to be correct.

Miami Beach Beckons

Miami Beach has had more words written about it and its history than any other city of comparable size in America, with the possible exceptions of Atlantic City and Las Vegas, and now, with the city approaching its 100th birthday in 2015, it remains one of the most talked-about cities and most desirable and exciting destinations in the world. That, in 1925, was exactly how Roddy Burdine looked at it, though not as a place to enjoy as a resort or for a vacation, but rather as a place to do business, for it was obvious even at that time that the opportunities offered by the ten-year-old city for a commercial opportunity during the winter season were limitless.

How was it that Burdine chose to open the firm's second store on Miami Beach in 1926? Why not in Miami Shores at the hotel being developed at the corner of Northeast Fourth Avenue, Grand Concourse and Ninety-sixth Street by Ellen Spears Harris and Hugh Anderson and their Shoreland Company? After all, it was they who bought the old Collins Bridge (then the longest wooden bridge in the world) from the Carl Fisher group and built, in its place, the Venetian Causeway and its beautiful islands. They then moved north with plans to build a mid-bay causeway and develop a six-hundred-acre recreational island named Miami Shores Island that they would connect to the mainland with a Grand Concourse. Why not Spears and Harris?

Why not in Coral Gables, being laid out and built by former citrus and produce farmer and area land developer George Merrick as only the second

When the Roney Plaza was opened, early in 1926, it was the talk of the nation, and Burdine's reaped the publicity, it having opened its first branch, a winter-season store that would operate only during the months the hotel was open. Burdine's remained in the Roney Plaza until it opened its year-round store on Lincoln Road in 1936.

An aerial view of the Roney Plaza shows the famous Roman Pools, which began life as Carl Fisher's (the founder of Miami Beach) Fisher–St. John's Casino. The Roman Pools were easily recognized because of the windmill that had been built at the east end of the pool deck and that is visible in this image. Shoppers could avail themselves of not only the shops in the Roney, including Burdine's, but also the Roman Pools.

completely planned city in America? (Washington, D.C., was the first.) And why not put the store specifically in the Bowman-Miami Biltmore Hotel, which Merrick was having built by famed hotelier John Bowman?

Burdine could have considered the planned hotel at Merle Tebbetts's Fulford-by-the-Sea (now North Miami Beach) or in Harvey Baker Graves's Sunny Isles, where an expensive gaming and bathing casino had already been built, with a major hotel planned. He could have even looked west to the Curtiss-Bright cities—Hialeah, Miami Springs and Opa Locka—but he didn't. And when the obvious question is asked, the answer is always the same: because the sun, surf, sand, bathing beauties and city itself made Miami Beach the one and only choice for a second Burdine's store.

Miami Beach had its modern-day origins in 1882 as a coconut plantation, purchased from the original owners (who had paid thirty-five cents per acre) for the princely sum of seventy-five cents per acre. When the coconut plantation failed, it was sold to two men from Merchantville, New Jersey, whose names would become revered in Greater Miami's history: John S. Collins and his son-in-law, Thomas Pancoast. Collins and Pancoast converted the property into a highly profitable avocado/mango/papaya/potato farm, building a canal across the island and digging out a turning basin for their barges so that they would not have to pay the tariffs imposed on them by Avery Smith for the privilege of being able to ship their goods via Smith's Biscayne Bay Navigation Company ferries over to the mainland and the FEC docks for transshipment to the northern markets. (The canal is today known as the Collins Canal, which parallels Dade Boulevard on Miami Beach. The turning basin, built directly across from where the Roney Plaza Hotel—the eventual site of the Miami Beach Burdine's store—would be built about twenty years later, is today known as Lake Pancoast.)

Collins and Pancoast recognized that, even though they were doing well as farmers, they likely could and would be better off as real estate magnates. Recognizing the rising value of land on the mainland, they decided to subdivide and sell their property, by that time known as Ocean Beach. However, in order to do so, there would need to be a bridge built so that they could accommodate all of those newfangled horseless carriages that would, with their owners, want to see the property. They then set out in 1911 to construct the longest wooden bridge in the world, from what is today's Northeast Fifteenth Street and North Bayshore Drive on the Miami side to

Right: The damage to the Roney from the 1925 hurricane is evident in this picture, taken from the east end on Twenty-third Street and looking west along the hotel's south side. Sand was piled more than six feet high in some places, and the damage was substantial.

Below: This very rare post-hurricane postcard shows the men and equipment working to remove the sand from what the author believes is Collins Avenue. The building behind the crane and the truck looks like the Roney employee's dormitory.

today's Dade Boulevard on the Miami Beach side, across a completely open bay without any intervening islands, with the singular exception of what was then known as Bull Island (sometimes "Bulls Island") and is today's Belle Isle, the first island to the west of Miami Beach on the Venetian Causeway.

At some point during the construction, whether it was one-third or half of the way across, Collins and Pancoast ran out of money, and that is the beginning of the story of confluence and coincidence that would eventually bring Roddey Burdine to Carl Fisher and Jim Allison's Miami Beach and, specifically, to Newt Roney's magnificent new Roney Plaza Hotel, but to reach that point it is necessary to tell the rest of the story.

Collins and Pancoast returned to New Jersey and began to cast about for financial assistance for their project, being met, for the most part, with negative reactions if not derision. "After all," chided some of the well-reasoned replies, "why would I want to invest in a bridge over to a farm when there is a perfectly good ferry service operating?" It should be noted that this was before the laws were put into effect that prohibit private entities from owning bridges across navigable waterways.

Finally, the two men ran into (or were introduced to—the story is not entirely clear) the man who would be the connection to their savior in regard to bailing them out: John S. Levi, a yacht broker. Interestingly, even at that time, the very wealthy enjoyed indulging themselves with expensive toys, such as their own private yachts or railroad cars, and Collins and Pancoast hoped that Levi, who certainly knew wealthy people, might be able to introduce them to an investor for their bridge.

It was at just about that time when two men from Indianapolis, Carl Graham Fisher and James Allison, owners of "the brickyard" (as the original Indianapolis Motor Speedway was then called), sold one of their inventions to Union Carbide. In the early days of the automobile, anyone wishing to drive at night had to attach lanterns to the front of his vehicle, and Fisher and Allison, through their Prest-o-Lite Company, had invented something that is today taken for granted: a switch on the dashboard connected to lights that were already attached to the front of the vehicle. It was at the time a major breakthrough in automobile technology.

Union Carbide felt that this switch was the future (it would, after all, enable drivers to use their automobiles at night) and that all automobiles would be so equipped. With that belief, Union Carbide handed Fisher and

Recovering quickly from the hurricane, Newt Roney ordered a new pool and cabana club built, and for many years, that was the place to be seen both during the season and in the summer; even though the hotel was closed from early spring until late fall, cabanas were rented for the summer season and the pool and a snack bar were kept open.

Allison checks for $5,633,000 each (imagine what this amount of money was worth at that time). The men remained friends and partners, so much so that they even remained partners in the investment in what would become Miami Beach.

Fisher decided that he wanted a yacht, and naturally and coincidentally he was introduced to none other than John S. Levi. Working with Levi, Fisher commissioned a yacht to be built in Cairo, Illinois, on the Mississippi River, and upon its completion, Fisher and Levi took it for a shakedown cruise to New Orleans. At that point, Fisher planned to have Levi take the boat to Jacksonville for maintenance, but one of the engines malfunctioned, and Fisher left Levi to have the boat repaired and to meet him in Florida's hub city. With the errant engine back in working order, Levi proceeded to take the boat south through the Gulf of Mexico, planning to pilot it along the Gulf Stream and up the east coast of Florida to Jacksonville. However, once he was parallel to Miami, the place he had heard about from Collins and Pancoast and that he knew was already being referred to as the "Magic City," he decided to bring the yacht into the Miami River and take a look for himself. Suffice it to say, he was stunned by what he saw, for it was gloriously beautiful and unlike anything he had ever seen before.

Levi wired Fisher, and though the telegram is no longer extant, it said, in effect, "Forget Jacksonville. Meet me in Miami." This Fisher did. Without going into the lengthy details, Levi introduced Fisher to Collins and Pancoast, and Fisher asked them what it was they wanted. With great excitement, the two men took Fisher to the site of the temporarily dormant bridge construction and then, via the ferry, over to Ocean Beach. Fisher did not say much that day, but one of the famous and true Miami Beach stories, recounted by Jane Fisher in her book *Fabulous Hoosier*, is that when Carl got back to the home that he and Jane had rented on the Miami side, he was flushed with anticipation. Jane recounted, "Carl said to me, 'Jane, I couldn't believe it. It was the damndest thing I have ever seen. This little Quaker is seventy-five years old, an age at which most men are ready to lie down and die, and he is ready to start a whole new chapter in his life!'" Jane knew then that Carl was ready to start a whole new chapter is *his* life.

Within just a few days, Carl arranged to give Collins and Pancoast the funding they needed, but not as a loan. Rather, he would accept land from them, 222 acres, and then buy another 55 acres, and that was the beginning of what would, four years later, become the town of Miami Beach.

And what does that have to do with the Burdine's story? Everything, for without some background, the recounting of how and why the Burdine interests opened a branch on Miami Beach would just be, as the story has been each time it has been told in the past, no more than two brief paragraphs, when in truth, it is a story of faith and trust in the future of Miami Beach and a separate story of Roddey's willpower winning out over the protestations of not only his brothers but also those of George Whitten, his trusted advisor, who believed that a store in a hotel over on the beach that would be open only in the winter could not generate enough revenue to make the investment worthwhile. Whitten, able to talk frankly and freely to Roddey, also pointed out that besides the rent, they would have to pay the costs of furnishing the store with its display tables, shelving, dressing rooms, mirroring and fixtures and arrange to have deliveries made on an almost daily basis to replenish purchased merchandise. While not pooh-poohing his brothers' and colleague's objections, Roddey, as president, made it quite clear that, with the builder of the Roney Plaza an excellent customer of the Miami store, N.B.T. "Newt" Roney was also willing to take a chance on *them*.

Newt Roney was another of Miami's early chance takers, investors, boosters and believers. According to Howard Kleinberg in his book *Miami: The Way We Were*, Roney purchased the huge piece of property—550 feet on the Collins Avenue and Atlantic Ocean sides and 400 feet of frontage on the Twenty-third and Twenty-fourth Street sides—from Collins and Pancoast. On January 31, 1925, with the great Miami boom nearing its apex, Roney announced his plans for the largest and most magnificent hotel ever to be built south of Palm Beach, where the Flagler System was operating both the Royal Poinciana and the Breakers. The news was electrifying, and it was also carried throughout the United States, Canada and Europe via the wire services.

The hotel debuted with a "soft" opening in January 1926 and then was opened to the public with massive publicity during the first week of February 1926. The hotel was designed by Schultze & Weaver, the architectural firm of the Waldorf-Astoria in New York City, the Breakers in Palm Beach and the Biltmore in Coral Gables. With its classic lines, the Roney Plaza was the grande dame of Miami Beach hotels until the Fontainebleau opened in December 1954. Guests included the Duke and Duchess of Windsor, Orson Welles, Rita Hayworth, Bernard Gimbel (of retailing fame) and Vincent Astor, among many others. Desi Arnaz was a Roney regular, performing and leading his orchestra in its showroom, while famed radio commentator and columnist Walter Winchell did many of his radio broadcasts ("Good evening, Mr. and Mrs. America and all the ships at sea…") from the Roney's nationally renowned Bamboo Room and Restaurant. The Roney was the first hotel on Miami Beach to offer cabanas, tennis on site and golf putting greens and instruction.

Roberta Morgan's *It's Better at Burdine's* relates that by the winter of 1925–26, Miami Beach had become *the* mecca of sun-seeking visitors and celebrities, with the Roney Plaza being the "in" place to stay. Unfortunately, a good bit of what Morgan wrote was either lacking in detail or completely incorrect. While the preceding sentences are factual, the statement that "Roddey Burdine was right on top of this boom, and decided to set up a small but stylish shop in the fashionable hotel, which became a haven of its own for those shedding their northern woolens for the fashions of the sun" leaves out the fact that while Roddey did decide to set up such a shop, it was only because of the fact that, through his friendship with Roney, an agreement would be worked out that would provide the store with the least possible financial exposure and allow the retailer to have the store open to the public only during the winter season, in concert with the months that the hotel was open for business. (In that era and, in fact, until just after World War II, almost every Miami Beach hotel was open during the winter season only, most of them from mid-December until no later than Easter, and the resort during the summer was equivalent to a "ghost town.")

The store carried only resort wear and accompaniments, with no hard goods of any kind. Roddey recognized the lure of Miami Beach and the aura it created, with tourists returning to the frozen north with their deep tans (in the days before concerns relating to skin cancer had surfaced). Wealthy easterners from Baltimore, Philadelphia, New Jersey, New York and Boston, as well as midwesterners from St. Louis, Chicago, Detroit and Cleveland, came in those days for "the season" rather than just for a week or two. When returning to their homes, it was very fashionable to show where they had been not only through the quite visible luster of their newly obtained tans but also by bringing back "something from Burdine's." That, to so many people at that time, became one of the hallmarks through which the traveler of the era was able to use to show that he or she was indeed a person of substance.

Although the opening of the Miami Beach store was certainly a bright spot for Miami's business community, given the situation following the capsizing of the *Prinz Valdemar* at the mouth of the turning basin of the Miami harbor on January 10, 1926, and its aftermath, the fact was that the "five terrible events of 1926" were and would be the harbinger of the Great Depression that would begin in October 1929. Suffice it to say, as Helen Muir wrote in *Miami, U.S.A.*, "Business was so poor that Burdine and Quarterman advertised a sale with 'dramatic reductions.'"

Newt Roney, who had been given the nickname "No Back Talk" (based on his initials), received a new moniker from the local newspaper columnists following the devastating events of 1926. Roney, who had been one of the great pioneers and, certainly on Miami Beach, one of the engineers of the great boom, suddenly found himself being referred to as "Nothing But Trouble" Roney.

Even with the business decline brought about by the five terrible events of 1926, there was still a strong belief that the "ship of business" could

CLUB BREAKFAST

SERVED IN ROOMS OR RESTAURANT

From 7 a. m. to 11 a. m.

NO ROOM SERVICE CHARGE

NO. 1   **60 CENTS**

Stewed Prunes, Grapefruit, Orange or Tomato Juice or Cereal

One Egg, any Style with Rasher of Bacon

Marmalade

Rolls or Toast   Tea or Coffee

NO. 2   **75 CENTS**

Stewed Prunes, Grapefruit, Orange or Tomato Juice or Cereal

Ham or Bacon and Eggs, any style

Marmalade

Rolls or Toast   Tea or Coffee

NO. 3   **1.00**

Grapefruit, Orange or Tomato Juice

Half Grapefruit   Sliced Orange

Stewed Prunes   Baked Apple and Cream   Sliced Bananas

Any Cereal with Cream

Ham or Bacon and Eggs, any Style

Griddle Cakes with Sausage

English Kippered Herring

Calf's Liver and Bacon

Marmalade

Rolls or Toast   Tea or Coffee

The "Burdine's era" at the Roney was a very special moment in time, and while it gave Burdine's even greater exposure to a completely new market, it also gave Burdiners the opportunity to enjoy the services of the hotel in which their store was located. This is a 1929–30 season menu, and as the reader will note, the breakfast selections, ranging from sixty cents to one dollar, were certainly great enough to satisfy any appetite.

be righted. To that end, Roddey and Whitten made the decision, for the 1928–29 season, to redesign the beach store and bring in Hiram Blakey as the store's manager. The store was completely remodeled, and new reed and bamboo furniture was brought in to give a feeling of comfortable informality, while the store was divided into six selling sections: a ready-to-wear area, a millinery department, ladies resort wear and accessories, men's and women's clothing and furnishings and, for the first time ever in that store, a department specializing in sporting goods (with a small but elegant assortment of luggage).

There is, as the reader may have surmised, still more to the Miami Beach Burdine's story, and that will be expanded on in the following chapter.

The Boom Busts and Burdine's Retrenches

The great Florida boom of the 1920s affected everybody in Florida, but primarily it was centered on the lower east coast, with the epicenter being Greater Miami. And when the bubble burst, it was equally colossal. But it didn't happen all at once. Rather, it was a series of events, as I tell my Florida history students at Barry University and Florida International University—the "five terrible events of 1926"—beginning with the capsizing and sinking of the Danish five-masted schooner *Prinz Valdemar* at the mouth of the Port of Miami's turning basin on January 10, 1926, completely blocking all shipping, and culminating with the horrific September 17 and 18, 1926 hurricane that was the harbinger of the Great Depression, which began three years later in October 1929 and led to the eventual closing of one of Burdine's two Miami stores.

The great boom, as discussed in the previous chapter, was a glorious time for the nation, for Florida and for Greater Miami—one that would never end, it was hoped. After all, business was so good and everybody was prospering and making money beyond belief, with Miami growing by leaps and bounds. But something did happen—actually a series of five events, beginning on January 10, 1926, shortly after the new year had begun.

The *Prinz Valdemar* was a 241-foot steel-hulled schooner named after Prince Valdemar of Denmark, and it was one of the last great ships of the sailing

This page: Two views show the terrible damage and destruction caused on the Miami side by the 1926 hurricane. The first allows the reader to understand how powerful the storm was, literally tossing boats out of the water and across the newly built Biscayne Boulevard, while the second picture is a close-up of a freighter, with broken coconut palms in the foreground and the shattered windows of Miami's newest hotels in the background.

ship era. While the ship was being used as a freighter, it was purchased by a group that planned to turn it into a floating hotel, this during the heady days of the great 1920s land boom. Somehow, and for some reason, the ship capsized right at the mouth of the turning basin of Miami's harbor, blocking all ship traffic incoming and outgoing. (This was years before Dodge Island was built; the Port of Miami then was a series of piers extending along Biscayne Boulevard from Northeast Sixth to Northeast Thirteenth Streets.)

Although the FEC Railway was newly double tracked, and even though the Seaboard Air Line Railway had reached Miami in January 1925, the FEC—barely able to manage the freight traffic pouring into Miami from the north and from Cuba before the double tracking, even with its newly laid second track—was unable to handle the immensely increased volume of traffic thrust on it following the capsizing of the *Prinz Valdemar*. The Seaboard, which came through Uleta, Opa Locka and Hialeah, was simply too far west at that time to provide much, if any, relief, and by February the FEC had placed an embargo on itself. Every siding was occupied between Jacksonville and Key West; with traffic able to move only if a freight car was emptied so another could take its place, and with twelve scheduled passenger trains plus extras operating each way each day between Jacksonville and Miami, the FEC could only allow food and medicine to come in unless the shipment had a letter of approval signed by then vice-president and general manager H.N. Rodenbaugh.

With that embargo, word began to filter out that there were problems in paradise and that building had ceased because construction material would not be carried south of Jacksonville by the FEC. With the negative publicity came concern by people who had purchased property as to whether they would be able to build homes or businesses given the issues and problems related to the transportation of the needed material. From and because of those concerns, many people began to default on their obligations, and developers such as Fisher, Merrick, Tebbetts, Anderson and Spears-Harris suddenly found that the flow of incoming revenue was beginning to dry up. With that, the news about conditions in South Florida became more ominous, and the situation became more difficult for the land magnates, who had salaries to pay and who were indebted to numerous suppliers for all of the construction material they had purchased on credit. At that point, the outlook began to reach a critical stage.

Although a bit earlier than the era of this chapter, this photograph of the original five-story Burdine building and store was of enough rarity that it had to be included. The store occupied only the first two floors, while the top three floors of the building were leased out as offices, in many cases to friends of Roddey Burdine. Names readable on the windows include attorneys T.N. Gautier and K.L. (or K.E.) Beyer, but of greatest interest to today's Miami and Burdine's historians will be the fact that the entire top floor, as noted by the names in all eight windows, was leased to Shutts, Smith & Bowen, attorneys (later Shutts & Bowen). On December 1, 1910, Shutts, with the backing of Henry Flagler, acquired the *Miami Evening Record* and changed its name to the *Miami Herald*, which he owned until it was purchased from him on October 25, 1939, by John S. Knight of Akron, Ohio.

As late summer passed and fall began, there was a modicum of hopefulness, and it was believed, with the FEC beginning to operate normally once again, that all of the problems could and would be resolved. That was only until September 17 and 18, when the fifth, last and most horrific of the "five terrible events" devastated all of South Florida and created such havoc and disruption (as well as an unprecedented death toll) that nothing thereafter could or would, for some years to come, begin to restore real prosperity to Greater Miami.

The September 17 and 18 hurricane killed more than four hundred people and devastated both Miami and Miami Beach. Burdine's auditors, in cooperation with the company's insurers, estimated the Miami store's damage to be more than $500,000, an enormous amount even for a store such as Burdine's, which by that time had become the single most patronized Miami-area retail store. The files of the now-defunct *Miami Daily News* are now housed at and maintained for online usage by the *Palm Beach Post*, and it is therefore, even without the ability to "cut and paste," fairly simple to access those online files, which provide no small amount of information and material on that terrible storm.

On September 18, 1926, the *Miami Daily News* managed to publish an "Extra," and under the headline, "Hurricane Hits Miami" and the subheads, the story began with two chilling paragraphs:

> *Miami was laid waste Saturday by a raging hurricane attended by a gale of more than 130 miles an hour velocity, and followed by one of the most disastrous tidal waves ever experienced on the Atlantic coast.*
>
> *Miami Beach was isolated from the mainland and no word has been received as to the effect of the storm there. It is feared that a monster tidal wave has swept across the entire island city.*

It was not quite that horrific, but as bad as the storm was, the Burdine's store actually sustained less damage than many of Miami's less structurally sound buildings. Many of them were simply destroyed, and the sixteen-story Meyer-Kiser building, a skyscraper not yet completed, was devastated so badly by the hurricane that several floors had to be removed following the storm. Things were almost as bad on Miami Beach.

The Burdine's store in the Roney Plaza, although not yet open for the new (1926–27) season, was flooded and the floors covered with sand. Photographs of the Roney following the storm show sand bulked against the south side of the building as high as the top of the first floor.

Roddey was out of the city when the storm hit and was notified by Vice-President and General Manager George Whitten of the damages. Unlike so many of today's managers or executives, Roddey's first concern was not for the building or the merchandise but rather for his store "family," and he immediately wired Whitten asking him to advise all store employees that Roddey's personal attention would be available to all employees immediately upon his return. He went on to state that he would help and assist any employee who required his assistance, noting that "the time for worrying about our store and Miami has passed" and that all managers and employees would work together to rebuild both the store and the city.

Burdine's led Miami out of the morass of the storm, first with positive and encouraging advertising and then by investing in the city and the store, helping to rebuild both and assuring all Miamians that Burdine's

This modern age has taught us to depend upon specialization for the ultimate accomplishment—in the arts, in science and in fashion.

Burdine's Specialization brings you

SUNSHINE FASHIONS

AMERICA'S SMARTEST RESORTWEAR

No longer does the fashion-wise woman select her entire resort wardrobe before reaching Florida. Since the winter vogue, down south, later becomes the summer mode for all America, Society is more reluctant, at this season than at any other time of year, to issue its decree of approval. Thus, no matter whence its pre-season influences, the resort mode really originates at Miami, Miami Beach and Palm Beach . . . . and advice received in even the very best of the "stores back home" is often contradicted by Fashion's final acceptance of "what shall be worn." For thirty years Burdine's has been the style leader in Florida's watering places. It is only natural that Sunshine Fashions, Burdine's exclusive creations and adaptations, offered only at its main Miami store and three ultra-smart shops, should come to be known as "America's Smartest Resortwear." So definite is the effect of Sunshine Fashions in the style trend for the southern winter and the following summer everywhere, that to be correct in her apparel the voyageuse must await Burdine's interpretation of the mode . . . . making her selections as the season progresses.

BURDINE'S

MIAMI (2 STORES)
MIAMI BEACH
PALM BEACH

CREATORS OF SUNSHINE FASHIONS

Burdine's February 1930 *Vanity Fair* magazine ad appeared with renderings of all four stores at the bottom, featuring "Sunshine Fashions" and "America's Smartest Resortwear" at the top.

and its employees would do everything necessary to assist the city in returning to normalcy.

Through good fortune, the Bramson Archive has become the repository of a number of copies of the company's monthly employee magazine, the *Burdynamo*, and several of the 1927 issues are highly enlightening as to what Roddey, his brothers and George Whitten either were doing or planned to do following the '26 hurricane. One of their innovations was to open a rooftop restaurant, which was, according to the *Burdynamo*, the first restaurant under a canopy on a rooftop in the United States.

One Burdine's researcher wrote that "the seating capacity was 1000"; given the size of the city, the building, the square footage of the roof, the space needed for kitchen, dish and pot washing facilities, the coolers, the freezers and the food and supplies storage, as well as the potential business, this would seem to have been beyond belief. It is much more likely that the statement meant that the roof restaurant could serve one thousand meals a day and not that the seating capacity itself was one thousand, although a company-issued postcard of the era (circa 1926–27) carries the following printed message on the back: "Burdine's roof restaurant on the sixth floor of this building is a gathering place for Miamians and visitors who seek a delightful place for dining. *It has a capacity of seating 1000 guests at one time* [emphasis added]."

However, that particular researcher's further comments regarding the rooftop restaurant support the author's questioning of the seating capacity, for after stating operating statistics indicating that the restaurant daily served, among other items, one hundred gallons of coffee, fifty gallons of tea and twenty gallons of milk, she wrote that "the staff was able to serve 400 lunches at noon within an hours notice," which would clearly indicate that they could serve as many as one thousand meals a day but *not* that the restaurant had a seating capacity of one thousand. Photographs of the store and of the rooftop, shown in this book, would tend to support those comments as a correction.

There is further reason to question the statement, primarily because on this card the store is shown extending north and south from Flagler Street to Southwest First Street and *east* from the corner of Miami Avenue and Flagler Street. The problem with the image is that it has clearly been doctored: the Biscayne Hotel, until purchased in 1936, occupied the southeast corner of Flagler Street and Miami Avenue, but on this card the hotel is shown to the *east* of the store, clearly an instance of artistic license but probably easily overlooked by anyone other than Miami memorabilia and postcard collectors.

By June 1927, a scant nine months following the worst hurricane to have ever hit Miami up until that time, Burdine's was rededicating itself to excellence. In May of that year, a major and extensive remodeling campaign was launched. Whitten was quoted as saying that "[it] will eclipse anything heretofore undertaken. Departments are being changed overnight, shifting from one floor to another, in order that each department may be relative to departments of similar nature."

The June '27 (volume 2, no. 1) issue of the *Burdynamo* was laden with optimism, the lead article in that issue titled "Burdine's—Keeping Pace With Miami" and noting that the Flagler Street wing was being remodeled through the tearing out of the second floor, "which now gives the main floor a splendid height. The ten massive columns in this section will be finished in travertine and the ornamental capitols will be decorated in pastel shades to harmonize with other decorations." The floor in that section was to be laid with black-and-white zenithern blocks, and "[m]assive sliding doors of oak [have] replaced the old style doors at the main entrance." The next sentence, however, is completely confusing: "During the day these doors slides [*sic*] back out of sight between the walls."

There is a great deal more in the way of department changes and relocations shown, including information regarding the book department, the pastry section, the service department, the rug and drapery department, the luggage department, the Victrola department (phonographs that today, except as antiques and conversation pieces, no longer exist), the lingerie section and many more. A new fire sprinkler system was installed, and the article concludes with the advice that while Burdine's was not only one of the largest department stores in the South and was the southernmost department store in the United States, the store also had "a big challenge to do big things in the mercantile world, especially here in southern Florida, and with the army of loyal employees of this store we will continue to progress and keep pace with Miami—and with Florida." This statement would prove, about forty years later, to be eerily prophetic, as Burdine's became the largest and single most recognized department store chain in the South and one of the largest in the nation.

At the same time that the improvements were being made to the Miami store, Newt Roney and George Whitten worked hand in hand to restore the Miami Beach store, which, although a bit later than usual, opened in time to serve hotel guests and other customers for the 1927 season. Although business was fairly good, there was a sense that there had been a decline in both optimism and the public's purchasing power since the 1926 hurricane. Keeping a strong hand and an even stronger public belief in the future for Miami and the stores, Roddey instituted a new line exclusive to Miami Beach (although it would later go into other stores) called "fun-in-the-sun wear," which held up quite well in the Roney store.

In 1928, several positive moves were made in terms of increasing Burdine's already forward-looking thinking. Neither the Burdine brothers nor George Whitten thought, felt or believed that the store did nothing more than serve a winter tourist town—they acted in a manner that would have done major northeastern and midwestern department stores proud. The "big" stores had, for several years, sent merchandise buyers, particularly those in the clothing lines, to Europe to seek out the newest fashions and finest fabrics, and this is what Burdine's started doing in 1928.

A series of fashion shows was begun, instituting a Burdine's tradition that would continue for close to seventy years, both in the store and at various locations in the Greater Miami area, especially when major women's organizations requested them or national conventions wanted to have activities directed toward the women who, single or accompanying their husbands, were attending those conventions.

Advertising in Miami's newspapers continued unabated. A marvelous (in retrospect) ad in the *Miami News* of May 25, 1928, allows us a glimpse not only of head-covering fashions but also of the prices and availabilities of other clothing items: "350 Women's Smart Hats," the ad told us, were available during "May Event No. 19" for the special price of $4.00 each. Men's neckties were $1.00, while boys fine shirts were on sale from $0.79 and up.

The store's marketing department, typically right on top of the newest methods of mass communication, won approval to begin a radio program on Miami's and Florida's first radio station, WQAM, which originally went on the air in February 1921 using the call letters WFAW. However, in 1922, the *Miami Metropolis* ended its participation in station programming, and in January 1923 the call letters were changed to WQAM. In 1926, the station increased its power to five hundred watts, making it tunable throughout what was then the Miami metro area. By 1928, the station's wattage was doubled to one thousand, and "QAM" became a CBS affiliate.

The program, which aired Monday through Friday at 9:45 a.m., was hosted by "Enid Bur," which spelled "Burdine" when rearranged. The program presented fashion news, shopping tips, information on new styles and store sales and even, from time to time, told listeners what the roof restaurant was featuring that week. It was a major breakthrough in communicating with the store's customers.

An early form of an in-house employee welfare organization had already been started, but in 1928, the Burdine's Employees Protective Association, which had a regular slate of officers made up of full-time company employees, started its own publication, the *B.E.P.A. News*, which kept employees up to date on store happenings, from special sales to awards won by various employees

Among Burdine's early competitors was the New York Department Store, owned by the Cromer and Cassel families; the name of the store was later changed to the family names. Some years later, it was sold to become the Mark Store and then Richards. Until the opening of Jordan Marsh, Richards was Burdine's main competitor. *Original photo by the late G.W. Romer, courtesy Miami-Dade Public Library Florida Collection.*

for outstanding service to new benefits being offered to them by management. It was, even in those still fairly early days, an excellent place to work.

By 1929, Burdine's was if not nationally known then certainly regionally recognized for its cutting-edge marketing techniques and willingness to experiment with new forms and methods of advertising. Even with Miami's and the nation's business in a slow decline, Roddey faced the future with optimism and that year copyrighted the marketing phrase "Sunshine Fashions."

By February 1930, the store was advertising nationally in magazines such as *Vanity Fair*, the small type at the top of a full-page ad above the headline stating, "This modern age has taught us to depend upon specialization for the ultimate accomplishments—in the arts, in science and in fashion." Below those words, in larger type was, "Burdine's specialization brings you," followed by the large headline of the ad, which read, "SUNSHINE FASHIONS." Below that was, "America's Smartest Resortwear," followed by the body of the ad. On the right was an artist's illustration in the Madam Doran mode of a slender model with a very low-cut V-neck top and an equally short beach dress standing on the beach, with a palm tree in the background. Renderings at the bottom of the ad showed the four stores then in existence: the main store at left and then, in smaller cuts from left to right, the Biscayne Boulevard, Miami Beach in the Roney Plaza and Palm Beach stores, the Palm Beach store apparently being located on Worth Avenue.

Even with the slight declines, the Phipps family, which had a substantial investment in Miami through their Bessemer Properties, invested heavily in both the city and its infrastructure, building with their own money an extension of Biscayne Boulevard—the plan was to reach both the exclusive Bay Point section and the area that would, after the bankruptcy of the Shoreland Company, become the Village of Miami Shores.

With the widening of Biscayne Boulevard to the north and the continuation of the streetcar service to and from Miami Beach via the then County (and now MacArthur) Causeway, Burdine's entered into an agreement with the developers of the beautiful new Art Deco building on the west side of the Boulevard that encompassed the full block between Northeast Thirteenth and Northeast Fourteenth Streets to open a store at the northern end of the building. Sears, Roebuck and Company, looking to expand into the Miami area even at that time, leased a larger section of the building at the southern end.

The opening of the new Burdine's store was a cause for joy and optimism. On December 4, 1929, just a month and a half after the great stock market crash that heralded the beginning of the Great Depression in the rest of the country, the opening, presided over by Roddey and William, was attended by most of Miami's politicians and civic leaders, all of them putting on their bravest and most optimistic faces, but each of them, in his or her heart, knowing that difficult times were ahead.

The stock market crash of 1929 sealed the nation's fate, as the Depression, which had seen its harbinger in 1926 in South Florida, would begin in earnest in October, but 1929 in general was not a good or happy year for the Burdine family. The matriarch of the Burdine clan, the brothers' mother, Mary, passed away on June 9; son Freeman, at the time the treasurer of the corporate entity, also died in 1929.

Mary was known and loved by almost every Burdine's employee, and upon her death, George Whitten, representing the family and the store's management, announced, "Out of respect for Mrs. William Burdine, the store will be closed for the remainder of the day today and tomorrow and business will not be conducted. All employees will be welcome to attend Mrs. Burdine's funeral." It is not known what actions were taken to commemorate Freeman's death, but it can probably be safely assumed that there was some kind of memorial held for him.

In the spring of 1930, with business declining due to conditions brought on by the Depression (which, at that point, was only in its first months nationally), Miami's publicists came up with a new slogan: "Stay through May!" Although Miami and Miami Beach typically emptied out by early to mid-April, the city fathers knew that something had to be done to encourage business into the late spring and even the early summer.

In *Miami, U.S.A.*, Helen Muir noted that the slogan was more than a slogan:

> *It was a desperate invitation to tourists to remain through one of the most inviting calendar months in South Florida and with it recent plans to attempt to develop a summer tourist season.* [This was, at that time, unheard of in Florida; there simply was no such thing.] *The Clyde Mallory Steamship Line announced reduced rates* [which the Florida East Coast Railway had done every summer for years]. *So did hotels and apartments. The indefatigable Ev Sewell asked for five and ten dollar offerings from merchants in order to publicize summertime Miami. In the spirit of the movement Pauline Burdine scheduled a summer fashion show.*

The idea of almost anything happening in Miami (or Miami Beach) other than the main Burdine's store remaining open to serve residents (similar to the Flagler System keeping the pool at the Royal Palm Hotel open in the summer for the use of the locals, even though the hotel was closed from early April until late December) was almost earth-shattering—Mrs. Burdine's graciousness in scheduling a fashion show out of season was therefore almost revolutionary.

The wording of Burdine's advertising at the end of the 1920s and into the early 1930s was close to genius. Consider the impact that the words in this *Vanity Fair* ad would make on the wealthy women of the era or even those of the middle class who could afford a South Florida vacation:

Sunshine Fashions and the Florida Store

No longer does the fashion-wise woman select her entire resort wardrobe before reaching Florida. Since the winter vogue, down south, later becomes the summer mode for all America, Society is more reluctant, at this season than at any other time of year, to issue its decree of approval. Thus, no matter whence its pre-season influences, the resort mode really originates at Miami, Miami Beach and Palm Beach…and advice received in even the very best of the "stores back home" is often contradicted by Fashion's final acceptance of "what shall be worn."

For thirty years Burdine's has been the style leader in Florida's watering places. It is only natural that Sunshine Fashions, Burdine's exclusive creations and adaptations, offered only at its main Miami store and three ultra-smart shoppes, should come to be known as "America's Smartest Resortwear." So definite is the effect of Sunshine Fashions in the style trend for the southern winter and the following summer everywhere, that to be correct in her apparel the voyageuse must await Burdine's interpretation of the mode…making her selections as the season progresses.

Even with that kind of wonderful advertising, and with the company doing its best to make the new store successful, the timing of the opening—almost perfectly coinciding with the onrush of the Depression, the falloff in business and the near complete emptiness of the town during the late spring, summer and most of the fall—combined in a near perfect maelstrom of business reversals. In 1932, after less than three years of operation and with little notice or fanfare, as the country was enduring its third year of a depression that would last for another seven, the anguished decision was made by the management board to close the store. With that closing, Burdine's would not have a second store within Miami's city limits until the opening of the short-lived store in the Mayfair shopping center in Coconut Grove in the 1980s.

Sunshine Fashions in the Depression

While another of the casualties of the Depression was the Palm Beach store, which was closed by the company in the early 1930s, the firm, with Roddey's and George Whitten's strong guiding hands at the helm, steered the two remaining stores through the Depression without showing any red ink, an incredible feat given the decline in business.

In 1930, Burdine's sales totaled $5.0 million, a substantial sum for that era, but by 1933, the year's sales had dropped by $2.3 million, yet even with a nearly 50 percent decline, Burdine and Whitten, shepherding their funds carefully and doing all they could to encourage business, still managed to eke out a net profit and finished the year in the black.

One of the marketing department's promotional tools was the use of "cheesecake," featuring pretty girls in abbreviated (for the era) bathing suits running down the beach, stretched out on a seawall or lolling against a coconut palm. This genre began when Carl Fisher, Miami Beach's primary developer, brought in the great New York PR man, Steve Hannagan, to help him sell lots on Miami Beach. Although there had been minimal interest up until that time, Hannagan hit on the idea of taking photos of the girls in their bathing suits in the dead of winter and then sending the photos by wire service to every newspaper in the country east of Kansas City. (That location chosen because the Frisco Railway, in conjunction with the Southern Railway and the FEC, ran a train to Jacksonville called the "Kansas City—Florida Special" that featured, in the winter, through coaches and Pullman sleeping cars all the way to Miami.) They featured cut lines such as, "It's December 22, and it's 79 degrees in Miami!" or "Surf bathing is a delight in January in Miami Beach." One of Hannagan's best lines was, "Miami Beach: Where summer spends the winter!" Needless to say, the country gasped in amazement when it saw the pictures and took the bait, hook, line and sinker, people making their train reservations to Miami as soon as they could.

The Burdine's marketing department grabbed on to the cheesecake routine, and the store's advertising featured beautiful young women in equally beautiful swim-, resort and beachwear and, in some cases, in the ocean or in the pool. Because of Burdine's friendship and association with Newt Roney, one of the most famous of the Burdine's ads featured a string of girls in the water at the edge of the Roney Plaza's famous swimming pool, with a tag line that read, "Models, resort wear and bathing suits by Burdine's Sunshine Fashions. Swimming pool by Roney Plaza Hotel, Miami Beach." With advertising such as that, and ongoing fashion shows both inside and outside of the store, Burdine's continued to keep a hold on the public's interest, even going so far as to divert their thoughts from the terrible business conditions around them.

As Florida, particularly southeast Florida, would learn from the Depression, it was quite fortunate that the state was not a manufacturing state, because the greatest job losses and the most distressing business declines were occurring in those states. While it was true that business did fall off in the four southeast Florida counties that were considered Burdine's prime trading area, the slide was not as bad as in the rest of America. Miami had the weather, and that would prove to be the key to a recovery that would begin years sooner than it did in almost any other place in the country.

Although a wonderful family man and a terrific father, Roddey's marriage to Zada, probably due to the time that Roddey had to dedicate to the store and to seeing that it would stay afloat during the Depression, was becoming increasingly troubled. In either 1932 or early 1933, they divorced. Roddey met Lillian Jennette Chapman shortly after the divorce was finalized and married her on September 14, 1933, with one son being the product of that marriage.

The year 1933 began with Miami looking as if it would be in the forefront of the recovery, but an incident occurred in Miami's Bayfront Park on

On December 4, 1929, in a great show of optimism, Burdine's opened its newest store on the west side of Biscayne Boulevard in the brand-new building that would house, first at its south end and eventually within the entire building (after Burdine's closed its store), Sears, Roebuck and Company. A beautiful store in a beautiful new building, Burdine's would close in 1932, a victim of the Great Depression.

February 15, 1933, that brought much negative publicity to the city. Early in the year, it was announced that America's new president, Franklin Delano Roosevelt, would visit Miami in concert with Chicago's mayor Anton J. Cermak and that they would appear together at the city's Bayfront Park, where they would give speeches in the park's amphitheater.

Twelve minutes before he ascended the stage, Cermak was photographed with Mayor Ev Sewell and Florida Power and Light Company's division manager, Henry H. "Hy" Hyman, the last photograph of Cermak taken before he was shot.

Once on the stage, before an excited and anticipatory audience, Cermak was shot and killed by a supposedly deranged Italian immigrant from Chicago named Guiseppe Zangara. While almost all sources and references to that event claim that Zangara was trying to kill Roosevelt and had missed, journalist Jay Maeder, who formerly wrote for the *Miami Herald* and the *New York Daily News*, has for several years been working on a book that documents the fact that Zangara had no intention of shooting Roosevelt but rather had been sent from Chicago to kill Cermak, who, as has been proven in the many years since the shooting, was on the payroll of Al Capone's rival, Bugs Moran. Although not directly related to Burdine's, the event did nothing to help Miami's image at the time.

Another view of the store, this from the north end of the building looking south. *Courtesy Don Boyd.*

The company immediately began to work with the city and with other firms on plans to improve business generally and to portray the city in a very positive light, and one of the many initiatives that came out of those efforts was the transition of the former Palm Fete to the Orange Bowl Festival, the very first game in 1935 featuring Bucknell University playing the hometown University of Miami.

Besides being a pioneer in the techniques of "suggestive selling" and increasing its business through assisting customers without appearing to be pushy or using "hard sell" techniques, the company noted that business was improving following the 1933 low point. The FEC, which had carded twelve Jacksonville–Miami round-trip passenger trains daily during the 1925–26 season, was down to only five by the 1933–34 season. As business increased, so did the train service, and by December 1935, the FEC had added a sixth train to its daily schedule. Roddey was in close touch with the FEC because the depot at 200 Northwest First Avenue was only two and a half blocks from the store, and top-level customers, those who were known to spend big bucks at Burdine's each season, were afforded complimentary rides to and from the station.

By the end of the 1934–35 fiscal year, which came on July 31, Burdine's sales, in an era when full meals in fine restaurants were $0.75 and rent in a decent apartment was $25.00 to $35.00 per month, had increased to $4.7 million, a not insubstantial figure when considering not only the prices noted in this paragraph but also that Miami and Miami Beach hotels were sending out flyers advertising that nightly per-person room rates were $1.50 to $2.50.

By the end of 1935, everything was on an upswing. A number of Jewish men from New York came to Miami Beach, liked what they saw and began construction of what would later be called Art Deco hotels. Construction meant jobs, and hotel construction meant that bricklayers, carpenters, masons, glass men, electricians and plumbers were put to work. To run the hotels, managers were hired who, in turn, brought in front desk people, maids and housekeepers, restaurant personnel, cleaning and maintenance staff and secretarial people, as well as physical therapy (massage) specialists and swimming pool and cabana club employees. Obviously, paychecks meant disposable income, and that meant improvements in business.

Roddey and George Whitten, seeing and sensing what was going on, realized that more and more people were returning to Miami, still known as the "Magic City." The two men, being acutely aware that business in the seasonal Miami Beach store had increased dramatically, made plans, beginning early in 1935, to open a full-service store on Miami Beach and had chosen as the site of that store the street that had attained the sobriquet of "the Fifth Avenue of the South": Lincoln Road.

The exact location was on the southwest corner of Lincoln Road and Meridian Avenue. When completed, the new building was a beautiful rounded-front Art Deco–style building, constructed for Burdine's with two floors. It carried a greatly expanded line of furnishings and accessories, although it excluded hard goods from the inventory, as space would not have permitted such items as furniture. The decision was also made to not include a food service operation in the store, as Lincoln Road, then in its original full bloom—with high-end automobile showrooms including LaSalle and Packard, a Bonwit Teller store, Saks Fifth Avenue and numerous jewelry, fine antique, china, linen and other quality goods establishments—had a wide selection of fine restaurants, including Russian and French cuisine emporiums.

While the opening, which took place in January 1936, was attended by numerous Greater Miami politicos, celebs and society types (as well as hundreds of normal folks), one face was conspicuously missing from the throng: Roddey Burdine.

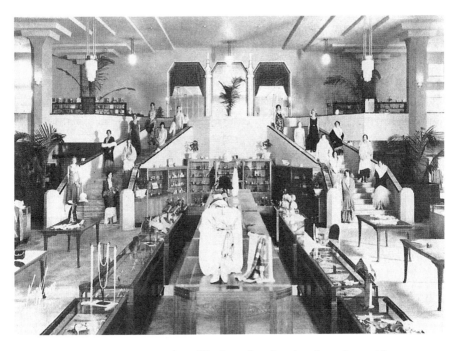

The Biscayne Boulevard store had a strikingly modern interior, shown here with saleswomen and models in the newest haute couture Sunshine Fashions. *Courtesy Don Boyd.*

With a very young child and a new wife, Roddey had become afflicted with what was then called "brain fever" but that was, in actuality, far more ominous. The term "brain fever" referred to what was most likely encephalitis. The cause of the fatal disease was unknown, and it was never specifically named, but in any case, Roddey died in St. Francis Hospital on Miami Beach's Allison Island on February 15, 1936. Miami's beloved Merchant Prince was only forty-nine years old.

The next day's *New York Times* carried a lengthy obituary on him, detailing all of his achievements, good works and accomplishments, and even lengthier tributes were paid by Florida newspapers, particularly the *Palm Beach Post, Miami Daily News* and *Miami Herald*, all of which, in addition to the obituaries, carried front-page stories.

So many of the important tasks that Roddey had engaged in outside of the business of the store were known only to a relatively small number of people, and many were surprised to learn that it was he who brought the first major golf tournaments to the area and that he had supported numerous sports, such as swimming and tennis. His contributions to various charities were, at the time, mostly unequalled in Miami.

The Miami City Commission and Dade County offices, almost all in the Dade County Courthouse, closed their doors on the day of Roddey's funeral and shut down in tribute to the man and his great work on behalf of the people of the city and the county. But the greatest tribute would come the following year, for on August 4, 1937, the almost brand-new Orange Bowl stadium was renamed Roddey Burdine Stadium to honor his memory and thank him posthumously for all that he had done for so many of all creeds and races.

Typical of the letters, wires, cables and other messages of condolence and sympathy was the one received by George's office from Harry M. Wolfe, company photographer of the Florida East Coast Railway. Apparently, he and Roddey had known each other quite well because Wolfe, as company photographer, spent a good bit of time in Miami, both before and after the September 2, 1935 destruction of the Key West Extension by that vicious hurricane. In his letter, Wolfe wrote, "My dear George: I am so distressed by Roddey's sudden passing that I am at a terrible loss for the right words…like

The interior of the main store, on Flagler Street, is shown here circa 1932.

all who knew him I will miss him greatly and although I will certainly make it a point to visit with you whenever I am in Miami on company business I want you to know that I will be thinking of him and all of his kindnesses."

Following Roddey's death, and through the terms of his will, his brother, William Jr., became the corporation's president. "Willie" and their dear friend, store vice-president and general manager, George Whitten, were named joint trustees of the estate and co-guardians of Roddey and Zada's daughters, Zada and Pat. Strangely, no mention is made in the Morgan book regarding Roddey's only son, Roddey Jr., who upon the death of his father could not have been more than a year and a half old; it is logical to assume, then, that unless Roddey's second wife did not want the same arrangements made for their son, Roddey Jr. was looked after in a comforting manner.

Unlike many of today's ironhanded micromanagers, who are afraid to cultivate young new executives in order to ensure the perpetuation of the business, Roddey felt exactly the opposite. Immediately upon his passing, his brother Willie (his name is sometimes seen as "Billie") and friend Whitten were prepared to immediately take the corporate reins, and they indeed moved quickly to continue the Burdine legacy.

On July 30, 1936, the company announced the purchase of the remaining portion of the Biscayne Hotel, the only thing that stood in the way of the expansion of the store west to Miami Avenue, which would allow the store to cover the entire block from Flagler Street south to Southwest First Street. A.S. Beck Shoes was on the ground floor of the Flagler Street and Miami Avenue corner and would later be moved across the street, to the southwest corner of Flagler Street and Miami Avenue, where it would remain for many years. Under Burdine's new ownership, though, the expansion was not carried out until following World War II, more than nine years later.

In 1936, the year that escalators were installed in the Miami store, the company netted almost $464,000 on over $5,609,500 in sales.

Between 1936 and 1938, extensive rebuilding and remodeling projects were carried out at a cost of $1.5 million, with the newly remodeled building opened to the public on November 13, 1938, complete with new departments and a special deluxe gift-wrapping service. The store was luxurious and exuded an air of elegance never seen before in a Miami retail outlet. The new Burdine's tearoom was actually similar to New York's famed "21 Club," which was not a club at all but rather a fine dining room. The

It was the height of the Depression, yet this 1935–36 winter season view shows two FEC passenger trains ready to depart from the downtown Miami depot behind two of the railway's 800-series steam locomotives. The Mark Store, formerly Cromer-Cassel and later Richards, is visible center left. Burdine's, to the east of the Dade County Courthouse (the tall building center right behind the trains) is not quite visible in this view.

tearoom became the luncheon home of not only shoppers but also a large number of downtown Miami business executives. One of the features of the time, and one that remained for many years, was the Men's Grill, which was actually located within the tearoom but that, at lunch, was reserved for male members only; it would not be until the mid-1970s that the bars were let down and women were permitted to dine there also.

Even with the new escalators, the elevators were upgraded, and beautiful young women in white gloves operated them. The store joined the Associated Merchandising Corporation in February 1938, allowing it to take advantage of a major department story purchasing and research organization, which at the time was presided over by Lincoln Filene of the famed Boston store group. AMC was made up of twenty-six high-level department stores, and with that affiliation, Burdine's was able to take advantage of expanded buying and fashion exchange and information opportunities.

With the completion of the renovations and rebuilding, Burdine's let the world know what it was truly about, and a 1939 national advertisement, which appeared in either *Collier's* magazine, the *Saturday Evening Post* or, possibly, *Life* magazine really ballyhooed the new store and its new look. Above a beautiful artist's rendering of the new store were the words, "New Home for Burdine's World Famous Sunshine Fashions," while below the rendering was a descriptive of the new Flagler Street store: "Ready now is a great, new Burdine store. Thrillingly, dramatically beautiful, it is an appropriate setting for the most exciting collection of Sunshine Fashions we have ever assembled. More so than ever these new Sunshine Fashions will preview nation-wide trends for next Summer in smart resort-wear and accessories. More so than ever you will find it fashion-wise to BRING YOUR TRUNKS—EMPTY!" At the bottom of the advertisement, on either side of the words, "Our Forty-First Year of Resort Fashion Leadership," are the year the store was founded, "1898," on the left and the year in which the ad was placed, "1939," on the right.

The firm was, absolutely and unquestionably, intent on being recognized nationally as the premier sport, swim- and resort wear emporium in America, if not on the face of the earth. All of the store's employees, all of the store's advertising and all of the store's marketing and promotional efforts tied in with and were completely supportive of that theme.

Burdine's, with an aura of exclusivity, glamour, quality and refinement, began to attract national attention as shoppers and visitors ranging from American congressmen and senators to the Duke and Duchess of Windsor were made to feel welcome and at home at "the Florida store." Of course, the visit by the former king of England always drew a crowd, and Mr. Whitten, with the cooperation of his department managers, made sure that he was undisturbed while shopping; to make things easier for the duke, who was serving as governor of the then British-owned Bahamas, truckloads of clothing and other items of interest were taken to the royal yacht, docked at the Port of Miami, right on Biscayne Boulevard.

On Tuesday, April 1, 1940, Miami was stunned by the news that the city's mayor, pioneer Everest Sewell, had died. While Sewell was beloved by many, the fact is that he was instrumental in destroying Miami's streetcar system and had accepted "gifts" or "gratuities" from a conspiracy of road builders, gas

Sunshine Fashions

One good reason for the soundness of that fashion advice — "Come to Florida — with empty trunks"!—

Fashion-knowing and fashion-watching America will attend—as usual—the annual Burdine Sunshine Fashion Show in Miami January 27th.

Here in the gayest fashion garden party of the year the summer fashions for all America are predicted and shown. And as Burdine's Sunshine Fashions go—in Florida this winter—so go fashions all over America months later!

Burdine's forecast exactly how much white —how much and exactly what colors—how much of precisely what fabrics—exactly the winning silhouettes. These Sunshine Fashion edicts are looked forward to and eagerly listened for by all fashion-sensitive eyes and ears.

BURDINES MIAMI

And be sure to note these interesting things about Burdine's Fashions: There's no price penalty to them—and the low prices here this year represent a new value-standard with the same high fashion and quality standard as always.

BURDINES MIAMI...CREATORS OF SUNSHINE FASHIONS

Depression or no, nothing was going to stop Burdine's from getting the word out, as this full-page January 1932 *Vanity Fair* ad shows. Noting, in the second paragraph, that "Fashion-knowing and fashion-watching America will attend—as usual—the annual Burdine Sunshine Fashion Show in Miami January 27th," the ad does give a nod to the need to be a bit frugal during those difficult days: "There's no price penalty to them—and the low prices here this year represent a new value-standard with the same high fashion and quality standard as always."

and oil companies, automobile manufacturers and tire and rubber companies to denigrate the streetcar system as "old-fashioned" and "noisy," as well as "slow," when nothing could have been further from truth. Much to the distress of a large number of Miami's residents, the last Miami trolley to take them downtown to the Flagler Street store operated on November 1, 1940.

Sewell was a close personal friend of the Burdine family—they had "grown up" together in early Miami—and of course, Ev's brother was John Sewell, Miami's third mayor and the author of *Memoirs and History of Miami, Florida*, which he updated after the assassination of Chicago mayor Anton J. Cermak in 1933.

With the end of the Depression, and business improving almost daily, Whitten and Willie again began looking north, as West Palm Beach was experiencing major growth; with the timing that is a hallmark of greatness,

Views of the store showing the Southwest First Street side are exceedingly rare, especially when they include both the store and a Miami streetcar. Looking east on Southwest First, this photo shows the awnings on every window on the south side of the store, likely indicating that this was era before air conditioning.

they decided to reenter a market that they had, unhappily, departed from in the early 1930s. In April 1941 in West Palm Beach, Burdine's opened its third store via the purchase of the former Hatch's Department Store, which was located in a modern, air-conditioned building on the corner of Clematis and Olive Streets. According to Morgan's *It's Better at Burdine's*, when Burdine's bought the Hatch store, it was doing $750,000 a year in sales, had twenty-three departments and 110 employees, including officers and managers.

Morgan added that Burdine's gave the store a face-lift by modernizing everything in the store, from windows, lighting and department arrangements to merchandising methods, and all employees were schooled in the Burdine's style and manner of increasing business by both suggestive selling and up-selling. Sales volume increased immediately, and the only nod to tradition

Sometimes sheer luck brings several Miami icons together in one photograph, and this is one of those wonderful images that does just that: Miami streetcar no. 232 is signed "W. Flagler St." and carries advertising signs for boxing at the Beach Arena and Gilbert & Sullivan's Mikado at the Lincoln Theater on Miami Beach, while a Dolly Madison ice cream truck sits next to the streetcar waiting for the light to change, both of them on Southwest First Street, with the south side of Burdine's on the left.

Even in the Depression—at least until the September 2, 1935 hurricane destroyed forty miles of the right of way—Key Westers would take advantage of special FEC Railway round-trip excursion fares, which would allow them to come to Miami on Friday, spend the night, shop at Burdine's on Saturday and return to the Keys either on Saturday night or on a Sunday train. One of the FEC's passenger trains en route from Key West is shown here.

that Burdine's had to agree to was that Mr. Hatch would be allowed to maintain an office in the store for the remainder of his life. The new store was an immediate success, and it was a fitting and incredible end to an exciting and sometimes tragic decade.

Events to come, however, would be out of the control of anybody in Miami (or West Palm Beach), and with the Nazi invasion of Poland on September 1, 1939, the world changed almost instantly. Britain and France declared war on Germany immediately following the invasion, "peace in our time" proving to be a sad illusion. While the "phony war" extended through the 1939–40 winter, Germany in the spring of 1940 attacked and overpowered France, the Netherlands, Belgium and Luxembourg in a matter of a few months, forcing the British army to retreat across the English Channel from a place known as Dunkirk. Fortunately for the rest of the world, Germany betrayed and attacked its ally, the Soviet Union, along an 1,800-mile front on June 22, 1941, in what was known as Operation Barbarossa. On December 7, 1941, the Japanese attacked the American fleet at Pearl Harbor, with the United States declaring war on Japan the next day and Germany declaring war on America several days later. Everything had irrevocably changed, and a new world was at hand.

World War II and
Looking to the Future

S uffice it to say, the war changed everything. Although the country was
beginning to return to financial normalcy, the war provided a stimulus
that restarted every type of production, put people back on trains, created
thousands upon thousands of job, stimulated purchasing and brought
an entire nation together. Although military installations were opened
throughout America, it *was* different in Miami because, essentially, Miami
and Miami Beach were taken over by the military, and the U.S. Army, Air
Force, Navy and Coast Guard became the central and driving forces to
everything that went on in South Florida.

The site of today's Fort Lauderdale–Hollywood International Airport
was the Fort Lauderdale Naval Air Station (from which two separate
groups of navy planes took off and disappeared, leading to the completely
false stories that it was because of the "Bermuda triangle" when, in fact,
it had been navigational errors on the part of the squad leaders that led
to the tragedies). Today, at the west end of the airport, a small museum
commemorates the naval air station and its flyers and is open to the public
on certain days of the week.

Palm Beach International Airport, today at I-95, Southern Boulevard and
Belvedere Road, was the Palm Beach Naval Air Station, and while no stories
of mysterious disappearances plagued that installation, it was as important

Just as the U.S. Army Air Corps took over Miami Beach, so did the navy and the Coast Guard do the same on the Miami side. With the *Miami News* building in the background, a navy squadron, standing right on Biscayne Boulevard at Northeast Fifth Street, presents arms during a drill, complete with fixed bayonets on the men's rifles.

as the Fort Lauderdale installation in terms of patrolling for German submarines in the Atlantic, as well as for military training.

The Florida Keys held several small Coast Guard stations, while Key West, after some years of quiescence in terms of military activity, bristled with U.S. Navy ships and personnel and a new naval air station at Boca Chica Key, just northeast of Key West. The army also had a small unit at Fort Taylor, but for those men, nothing was as enjoyable as enough leave time that would allow them to spend a couple of days in Miami. Homestead, a small farming community twenty-eight miles south of Miami and accessible by a two-lane road known as South Dixie Highway or U.S. 1—used as well for freight service via the FEC Railway line that had once gone all the way to Key West—would be the location of a major U.S. Army Air Corps (later U.S. Army Air Force) base.

But with all of the suburban military activity, Greater Miami was still *the place*. Most of the histories recounting World War II activities in the Miami area have concentrated on the U.S. Army Air Corps at Miami Beach, and while there is validity to recognizing what that service meant for and did to Miami Beach during World War II, the effects that the navy and the Coast Guard (and to a lesser extent, the Marine Corps) had on "the Miami side" were equally important.

NAVAL AIR GUNNERS SCHOOL
MIAMI, FLORIDA

While almost everything from World War II relating to South Florida is rare and infrequently seen, this piece of postal stationery from the Naval Air Gunners School in Miami has to rank at or near the top of the rarity scale.

Unquestionably, though, Miami Beach was the nucleus for military activities in Greater Miami. Whether the Miami Beach Chamber of Commerce sent a delegation to Washington to present the city as an ideal barracks/billeting/mess hall/training ground is a matter of speculation seventy years later, as there is no documentation known that such an event actually occurred; it is far more likely that, through Congressional staff and senators, the "powers that be" at Miami Beach asked their representatives to convey to the president and General George Marshall, the chief of staff, the fact that Miami Beach had the space, the beds, the dining rooms that could become mess halls, as well as, of course, the incredible weather that would allow training to be conducted on an almost year-round basis. The beaches would be ideal not only for physical training but also, as would be the case at what is now Bal Harbour, as rifle ranges. The U.S. military became acutely aware of Miami Beach, Miami, south Dade County, and the open land in northwest Dade County that would be ideal for airfield construction.

The U.S. Army Air Corps, beginning in early 1942, started to appropriate hotel after hotel at Miami Beach, and construction and renovation crews worked on an almost twenty-four-hour-a-day basis to prepare the hotels for a new usage and a new life as barracks, dormitories, mess halls, officers' and enlisted men's clubs and, perhaps most importantly, as classrooms, with numerous meeting rooms turned into teaching facilities not only for the air cadets but also for the men and women who would be maintaining the planes. In addition to the hotels being used for bunking and training, the Nautilus Hotel, on the west side of Miami Beach (that property is now a large healthcare facility) at Forty Second Street and Alton Road, was taken over for use as a military hospital.

Tens of thousands of recruits and volunteers poured in, and Miami Beach was completely transformed. Troops began marching on Washington Avenue, Collins Avenue, Lincoln Road and on the golf courses, and many extant photographs show the troops marching past the Burdine's store on Lincoln Road.

The navy's Miami-based subchaser training school is shown here.

Several United Service Organizations (USO) facilities were established, including a large one on the South Beach pier that, before the war, had been a recreation facility. It was later moved to the Tenth Street Auditorium at Tenth Street and Ocean Drive, and Miami Beach women, including numerous beauties from Miami Beach High, volunteered to serve as hostesses for the men, many of whom had never been away from their homes before. As was learned after the war, literally thousands of those men vowed that, if they made it through the war, they would return to Miami Beach.

The Miami Beach USO club was a warm and welcoming place. The girls served coffee and sandwiches, danced with the troops during weekend get-togethers and, in several cases, made plans for marriage after the war, many of the men returning to the city to live and open businesses thereafter.

Diesel-powered submarines *Bass* and *Bonita* are coupled together while they are docked at the Port of Miami. Note the connecting gangway joining the two boats so that sailors from the *Bass* could cross over to the dock and then walk or take a bus to Burdine's to do their shore leave shopping.

A number of those young women related to the author how, during the war, they would shop with the soldiers on, among other Miami Beach streets, Lincoln Road. Several shared stories of the warmth and kindness that the men were shown when they entered the various stores, Burdine's, of course, being a standout.

Restaurants were packed, and shops and stores did landmark business. While Miami Beach was wonderful and Lincoln Road was "exclusive," the fact remained that the most enticing shopping area in South Florida continued to be downtown Miami, and innumerable World War II photographs show soldiers and sailors either individually or with other military personnel/ dates walking on Flagler Street. Burdine's employees were certainly among those enlisting in the services, and one of the main tenets of the firm was that any person called to serve would, without question, have his or her job back when he or she returned.

Miami was also recognized for what it could offer to the military, and the U.S. Navy established its South Atlantic command in the Alfred I. DuPont Building, the former site of the Halcyon Hotel at the corner of Northeast

Second Avenue and Flagler Street. Admirals, captains and other ranking personnel worked around the clock in that building setting up training schools, arranging barracks for both men and women and working with the City of Miami to utilize streets, such as the beautiful (and very wide) Biscayne Boulevard, for marching drills and maneuvers. Bayfront Park, the location of Mayor Cermak's shooting, was also utilized constantly for that purpose.

At the same time, the Coast Guard, working in concert with the navy, did much of its training in Greater Miami, including establishing several small installations for ocean patrol. There are numerous fine photographs and postcards that show navy planes flying in formation over downtown Miami, and the city became used to seeing them in operation on a daily basis.

In south Dade County, in what is today called Richmond, the navy established a blimp base, and it was from there that those ungainly appearing but incredibly utilitarian flying machines set out in search of German submarines, which in 1942 and 1943 attacked 111 ships within the area of the south Atlantic command. With those attacks, which resulted in the

Three navy bombers in formation over the "Magic City" sometime during World War II. The middle plane is blocking a view of the Burdine's building, but the street going through Bayfront Park in the center of this image is Flagler Street, which led right to the store.

killing or wounding of 882 men, the navy established what it called the Gulf Sea Frontier, giving it responsibility for patrolling the entire Gulf of Mexico and all of the Atlantic east of the Bahamas.

Utilizing planes, ships and blimps, the navy and Coast Guard eventually prevailed, and by the end of 1943, the South Florida waters had become so hostile and so inhospitable to the German subs that they were forced to withdraw. It is, of course, quite likely that some of the men who were sent out in search of the subs had gotten their training at the navy's subchaser school, which at the time of the war was located right on Biscayne Boulevard in the area north of today's entrance to Dodge Island and is now known as Bicentennial Park.

Because of the submarine attacks, which a good few living Miamians well remember, having seen the burning ships just off Miami Beach or farther north, the military issued orders that all buildings on Miami Beach facing east and all buildings on the Miami side with windows facing Biscayne Bay would have to have those windows completely shaded at night so that the German submarines would not be able to use the light to see the silhouettes of the passing ships. Additionally, to further reduce the light exposure, the military issued orders that all automobiles being driven at night were to have the upper and lower parts of their headlights covered or hooded so that the slits, while still allowing other drivers to see oncoming cars, would not allow that light to disperse, making it impossible to be seen at sea.

Northwest Dade was a beehive of military activity. Within almost stone's throw from one another were four airports, all concentrating on military operations. The use of that area for airport purposes actually began when aviation pioneer Glenn Curtiss, who had purchased the land as part of his planned development of what would later be known as Opa Locka, gave part of the land to the City of Miami, the city naming it Miami Municipal Airport (at a time well before Miami International Airport came into existence). It was that airport that was later renamed Amelia Earhart Field, for it was there where she and Fred Noonan began their ill-fated attempt to circumnavigate the world. Parts of the runway remain visible, and the property is now a major UPS facility, as well as the main Hialeah police station, with a public park also on the grounds.

Shortly before he died in 1930, Curtiss gave the rest of the airfield property to the United States Navy, which built the Naval Air Station Miami, from which both lighter- (dirigibles and blimps) and heavier-than-air craft operated, including such famous ships as the USS *Akron* and the German *Graf Zeppelin*.

During World War II, NAS Miami was a major training center, housing six separate training bases. Part of the naval air station was transferred to the U.S. Marine Corps, becoming Marine Air Station Miami.

The Marine Air Station, on the site of today's Miami-Dade College North Campus, maintained a Marine Corps presence in South Florida, and the tower from that airport is still part of the Miami-Dade Campus. The other facilities were located to the west, and they were used by the navy and the Coast Guard, as well as by the U.S. Army Air Force, whose fliers were brought to and from Miami Beach each day by bus.

Just east of the Marine Air Station—on what is today Northwest 119th Street and was, until recently, the Westview Country Club—the Women's Army Corps (WACs), Women's Air Force (WAFs) and WAVEs (navy women) barracks, mess hall and club were established in the building that would later become the country club.

In addition to the subchaser school, the navy established a naval gunners school in Miami, while the Coast Guard continued to operate seaplanes

Marching on Collins Avenue. This view shows the troops below (south of) Lincoln Road, with the "Military Zone" sign prominent to the right of the marchers.

from Dinner Key in Miami's Coconut Grove. Young recruits poured into Miami every day, mostly on regular or special trains on the FEC or the Seaboard Air Line Railway, and they were met at the stations and brought immediately to their training destinations.

Numerous photographs show the servicemen in training. Among the most memorable, one shows a group of soldiers serving as kitchen police (KPs) and peeling onions with gas masks on while a cook is standing behind them observing their work. Another truly evocative image shows trainees shirtless in the broiling heat on the beach in Lummus Park on Miami Beach, many of them wearing only shorts but all of them wearing gas masks in order to learn to protect themselves against German or Japanese poison gas attacks.

Each of the flying group trainees was assigned to a class, and the big moment for any class was, of course, graduation day, when the soldiers received their commissions. After a few short days of R and R, enjoying Miami and Miami Beach and perhaps buying some things for family or girlfriends at the various stores on Lincoln Road or Flagler Street, they

Every major street on Miami Beach was used for drill. Here the men are marching south on Washington Avenue. The WPA-built post office is the building on the left with the cupola on it, while the building on the right housed, *from right to left*, S.H. Kress & Co. (now a retail store), the Strand Restaurant (later the Governor Cafeteria) and the Cinema Casino, which later became a movie theater. Beyond the Cinema was Burdine's earliest Miami Beach competitor, Morris Brothers Department Store. The building, sans awnings, is still extant and still in use.

were sent off to their ports of embarkation for theaters throughout the world, across the Atlantic or the Pacific, with a good few of them eventually returning to call Miami home.

Everybody did his or her part, and while sacrifices by the civilian population were great, the war gave the business community a much-needed shot in the arm, with stores such as Burdine's, though operating with a reduced staff, still doing everything they could to assist with the war effort.

On March 3, 1942, the County Causeway, which connected Northeast Thirteenth Street on the Miami side with Fifth Street on the Miami Beach side, was renamed MacArthur Causeway to honor the general who, at that time, was still defending the Philippines. Everything in Miami, just as in the rest of the country, was war-oriented.

In addition to Miami and Miami Beach being used as training sites and facilities, the area housed two German prisoner of war camps, one in South Dade County near the site of the Richmond Naval Air Station and the other at what would later become Belle Haven Pool and Trailer Park on Northwest Seventy-ninth Street near Thirty-second Avenue. The prisoners at Richmond worked mostly on that base or in the South Dade County agricultural fields, but the Belle Haven Park prisoners were transported daily to an officers' barracks and mess hall facility at what is today Ninety-sixth Street and Collins Avenue in Bal Harbour, the location of the elegant and exclusive Bal Harbour Shops.

Prisoners, in their uniforms with a large "P" on the back of their shirts, were bussed to the officers' area, where they served as maintenance and grounds people, cooks, waiters and cleaners. Several of them, whether at Richmond POW camp or at Belle Haven, returned to Miami to live after the war, perhaps becoming Burdine's regulars thereafter.

The war, though, did not cause Burdine's to become inactive in the fashion world, and its advertising was focused on producing styles that would not be perceived as unnecessary or beyond the bounds of wartime good taste.

With the Depression had come numerous cutbacks, among them size and print quality of the company's employee magazine. The *Burdynamo*, which had been published monthly in 1926 and 1927 (and possibly into 1928, although unfortunately, as with so much else in the store's history, there is no record of how many issues were published or when the last one was distributed), was replaced at some point in time by a typewritten, mimeographed, four-page, seven-inch by eight-and-a-half-inch newsletter that could be folded

"Cadence count" on the old Miami Beach municipal golf course again shows the cadets in close order drill. The tall building, right background, is the famous Shelborne Hotel, which opened in 1940 and which the military took over in 1942. Today considered "the place" to go and to stay on Miami Beach, with owner Russell Galbut sparing no expense to make the hotel the centerpiece of the region's hospitality industry, the hotel opened to rave reviews—and a quite expensive rate for the penthouse at the time: fifteen dollars per night from December through June 1941.

vertically and placed into employee pay envelopes. Fortunately for Miami and Burdine's historians, the complete December 14, 1942 issue has survived and is in the Bramson Archive. It is laden with good and happy news.

The front-page "headline" reads "Our Appreciation to All," and the news, while being "good," is very surprising, given that so many people by then, a year after Japan's attack on Pearl Harbor, were involved in the war effort and had left the employ of the store either to go into the military or to work at jobs that were crucial to the war effort. As important as Burdine's was, it was not "crucial to the war effort," hence the information in the employee newsletter for December 14, 1942, is extremely interesting, as it was quite likely that the huge majority of those hired were women:

> *We now have 1,658 people and on October 1st we had 886 people. This means we have increased our force by 772 people since October 1st.*
>
> *The cooperation of our old employees* [likely referring to their length of service] *is greatly appreciated and the new people are to*

be congratulated on their splendid efforts to help Burdine's retain their standards of service during this very busy season.

One year of war has made quite a few changes in our Christmas problems. It is even more important than ever that we urge customers to carry packages due to the restrictions on truck mileage. The delivery department has had a great many personnel changes; one thing this year we are using women helpers in delivery whereas last year we had all men. [That was something that was going on nationally, as men went into the service and women stepped up to take their places. It was most noticeable in transportation, particularly the railroad industry, where women became ticket clerks, conductors, trainmen (gender-neutral term) and even mechanics.]

Credit restrictions mean that all purchases will be billed through December and the bill is payable by the 10th of January.

Gift wrapping is not encouraged as of previous years due to the desire to save both materials and the peoples' time in less essential work.

Our Christmas decorations are less elaborate and some of the materials from last year have been used again.

We have had a good selection of Christmas merchandise but re-orders are not possible and some items which were plentiful a year ago have disappeared entirely.

We miss many familiar faces around the store and especially miss our men who are now in the service.

With the help of everyone, Burdine's continues to carry on.

The remainder of the newsletter mentions men (and women) in the service, including, among others, Fred Harrison, John Paul Fox, Ernest Nelson, Shorty Christenson (who was away from Burdine's for the first time in fifteen years), Bill Drennon, Jim Keith, Harry Pickering and many more. The bulletin continued with news of and about store employees and their families, and it is certainly a valuable and informative piece of historic Burdine's memorabilia. Unlike so much else of Burdine's that was lost or destroyed over the years, this piece has survived and provides us with a brief glimpse of the store, its activities, who its employees were and what was going on in the world immediately outside the Burdine's buildings in Miami and on Miami Beach seventy years before the publication of this book.

While there is some good and valid information contained in Morgan's book on Burdine's history, there are a number of errors that are so glaring that—given that at least one of them appears in that author's discussion of World War II and its effect on the Miami area and on Burdine's—they can and should be noted here.

It is obvious that Morgan was victimized not only with misstatements but also with at least half a dozen other completely false comments given to her verbally as factual that could *not* have come from any written source. It is possible that the author was purposely given them with the specific intent to deceive. While it would be easy for me to state that, as the writer of this history of the Burdine's empire, I don't understand why somebody would want to do something like that, the fact is that I do understand why somebody would have intentionally provided false information to Ms. Morgan: it is likely because such persons did not receive the contract to write the book themselves and felt slighted. Any Miami historian would instantly know that these "facts" were falsehoods.

Morgan wrote the following, and because she did not check the information that she had been given, I must suggest that, at this point, the reader should prepare for a hearty laugh: "But the war did not call a halt to either fashion or fun. In the October 14th, 1943 edition of *The LaRonde Tribune Times Dispatch* (price: two cents) a newspaper designed to promote the Fontainebleau Hilton's new LaRonde Room, there is the following headline."

The problem? The entire statement is pure nonsense. No small amount of blame or fault lies with her for not double-checking those so-called sources, no matter who they were or what their reputations were at the time, though the fault doubly lies with those who fed her the false information. Why is the quoted piece so completely false? I'll outline the reasons:

- There was never a paper named the *LaRonde Tribune Times Dispatch*, and the so-called price of "two cents" is, like the name of the paper, completely made up;
- The Fontainebleau Hotel was built by the infamous (and late) Ben Novack, of Catskill Mountains, New York and Miami Beach disrepute; the architect of the hotel was the great Morris Lapidus. The hotel *opened* in December 1954, more than eleven years after the "newspaper" named above was supposedly issued;

"Waren't much there!" The early Miami streets weren't exactly paved. Rather, they were surfaced with crushed white rock, and in the bright sun, the glare was close to blinding. Two years before William Burdine arrived, an unknown photographer made this view of what is today one of Miami's major intersections, Flagler Street and Biscayne Boulevard. But when the photo was taken, in 1896, Twelfth Street ended at what was then simply called "Boulevard," and that street was where, on the east, civilization ended, for one could literally jump from Boulevard into Biscayne Bay.

A view looking west on Twelfth Street shows a row of horseless carriages and the Biscayne Hotel on the west side of the store. The store would, slowly but surely, take parts of the hotel, eventually extending from where the vacant lot is just to the east of the store all the way to Avenue D (Miami Avenue), the hotel becoming just another Miami memory.

Above: Until the property was purchased by Roddey Burdine, the Biscayne Hotel stood on the southeast corner of Twelfth Street and Avenue D. While the building was substantial for its time, the empty lot next to (east of) it should be carefully noted, for it was on that lot that Burdine's would build the five-story building that would be called "Miami's first skyscraper." In 1936, after several expansions, the company purchased the remaining part of the old Biscayne Hotel, extending the Burdine's property all the way to the corner of what by then was Flagler Street and Miami Avenue on the south side of Flagler. Although they did not tear down the former hotel building and complete the current store on the east side of Miami Avenue until after World War II, the company's plans also included a long-term lease on the property on the west side of Miami Avenue, which later would be connected to the east side via a three-story sky bridge joining the buildings.

Left: This 1929–30 Roney Plaza promotional booklet, distributed nationwide by railroad ticket offices and travel agents, featured a drawing of a beautiful model, likely in a Burdine's swimsuit, inviting northerners to join her for the hotel's opening that season, perhaps a bit earlier than usual, on Thanksgiving Day.

This photograph, taken in 1911, shows the interior of the then brand-new "W.M. Burdine's Sons/In the Heart of Miami" store. Taken from the entrance door, the second-floor balcony is visible on both the left and rights sides.

"Up on the roof!" A view of the famous Burdine's tea roof, but sans canopy. When opened, the roof restaurant was called "the largest canopied restaurant in the country," which may or may not have been true, but removing all of that canopy when hurricanes were approaching must have been an extremely difficult and time-consuming task. Though no one today is certain, this view makes it appear as if the canopy has been removed and the diners are able to gain relief from the sun under the welcoming umbrellas. The diners, mostly women, are elegantly dressed, and the servers are in beautiful costumes ranging from Oriental to Middle Eastern.

Twelfth Street, Miami, Fla.,
Showing the New Burdine Building
and the Burdine Store.

Two front views of the new five-story store show the building with the "Burdine's: The Winning Store" slogan painted on the east side and then, later, with the sign on the roof.

Burdine's Sunshine Fashions were all the rage, and the Roney pool was often the site of advertising shoots for the store. Here a group of models poses in the latest swimwear, with two of the ladies adjusting the bathing suit being worn by one of the beautiful girls, while another woman sits at the sewing machine, ready to make any changes necessary to ensure a perfect fit.

Burdine's sport and swimwear was always in evidence at the Roney, particularly during the years when the Miami Beach store was located in the hotel. Here tourists enjoy their oceanfront cabanas, while the Roman Pools' windmill is quite evident in the center background of this photo.

One of the favored fashion show venues for Burdine's, even after the store was moved to Lincoln Road, was the Roney Plaza. These women, enjoying their luncheon in the hotel's Terrace Room, are looking forward to the start of a Burdine's Sunshine Fashions show, which will feature the latest sport and swimwear. Interestingly, the women were being served by their favorite waiter: the charming and handsome Moishe Poopick, who is seen on the right side of the first table closest to the camera telling the ladies what their dessert was going to be.

After the new building opened, Burdine's advertised itself as a "Popular Price Department Store," that sign being visible on the building just past the Biscayne Hotel, which is on the corner of Twelfth Street (Flagler Street) and Avenue D (Miami Avenue). The Biscayne Pharmacy Drugs sign extended out from the hotel. On the left side of the street is the Budge Hardware building.

For Miami memorabilia collectors, it just doesn't get any better than this: two exceedingly rare issues of the Burdynamo, the company's in-house employee magazine, for July 1927 and September 1927, each filled with company and employee news, photographs and useful and interesting information for employees. Purists will notice that the picture of the store has been doctored: Burdine's did not extend its building to the corner of Flagler Street and South Miami Avenue until after World War II.

Yet another view of Twelfth Street finds us standing on the north side of the street looking west from just west of Avenue C, today's Northeast First Avenue. This view is significant for many reasons: cars parked on both sides of Twelfth Street; John and Ev Sewell's clothing and shoe store on the immediate left; and Rector's Café several buildings farther west on the left side of the street, followed by the Kress Building and then Burdine's. The Hotel McCrory is on the right, just past the balconies closest to the camera.

A very rare circa 1928–29 view taken on Flagler Street from west of the store looking east shows a Miami trolley boarding passengers on the corner of Miami Avenue. Florsheim Shoes is on the southwest corner of Flagler Street and Miami Avenue, and the Biscayne Hotel sign is on the canopy just west of Burdine's.

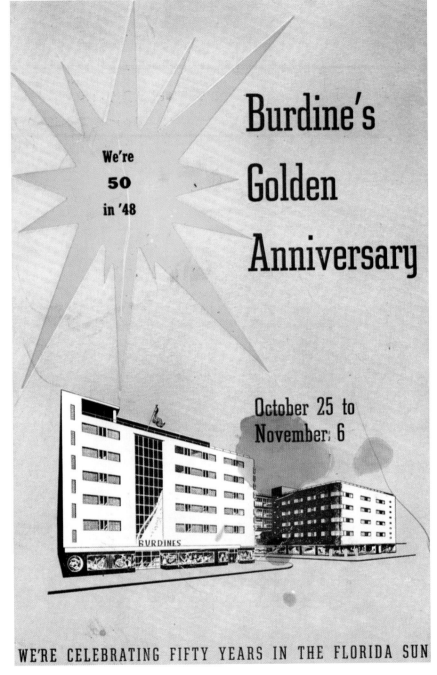

Burdine's Golden Anniversary

We're 50 in '48

October 25 to November 6

WE'RE CELEBRATING FIFTY YEARS IN THE FLORIDA SUN

The store's golden anniversary was celebrated from October 25 through November 6, 1948, a joyful week of events memorializing the firm's history. This was the menu for the Pioneer's Club dinner, which was held on October 20 of that year and was a kickoff to the anniversary week. For Miami's centennial in 1996 and the store's centennial two years later, sadly and regretfully to report, they did so little that "next to nothing" would be both a fair and an adequate descriptive.

Seasons Greetings

CHRISTMAS 1948

As Burdine's Golden Jubilee Christmas draws to its climax, it gives me a very real pleasure to send you this personal message of greeting.

You have come through our Fiftieth Christmas season in true Burdine manner, serving our many customers cheerfully and well.

Your fine spirit of cooperation is much appreciated and I want to take this opportunity to thank you for a year of fine service and wish you and yours

A very merry Christmas.

Geo. E. Whitten

Christmas 1949

Christmas is almost here again, and it gives me great pleasure to send you my personal greetings and good wishes.

As this busiest of all seasons comes to a close, I feel that every single one of you deserves a very special word of thanks and appreciation for the excellent way that you have handled your work, and the cheerful service you have given our customers.

May your Christmas be filled with everything good and may the New Year bring you happiness and success in every way.

Geo. E. Whitten

The war, thankfully, was over, and for the Christmases of 1948 and 1949, George Whitten sent these heartfelt season's greetings messages to each and every Burdine's employee.

In all his neon glory, Santa greeted Miamians on the Burdine's sky bridge from 1950 until the mid-1960s, and his yearly appearance told Miamians that the Christmas shopping season had begun in earnest.

The new Lincoln Road Miami Beach store, which opened in 1936, saw U.S. Army Air Corps marchers almost every day beginning in 1942. The store is about a block east, with the troops marching west. The closed-for-the-summer Bonwit Teller store on the left is just past the two-story building with the Lloyd's sign on the balcony above the cantilever

Marching on Collins Avenue. This view shows the troops north of Lincoln Road, with still famous Miami Beach hotels the Raleigh, Grossinger (later the Delano) and the National on the left.

Flagler Street at night, circa 1953, looking east from the corner of Miami Avenue, Budge Hardware having been supplanted by Crosby Shoes. The large Seybold Arcade neon sign is above the shoe store, facing Burdine's.

From just north of Flagler Street, looking south on Miami Avenue, the three-floor sky bridge connecting the two Burdine's buildings is quite prominent, while everything on the shoe store sign remains the same, except the name of the store.

The Fort Lauderdale store was located at South Andrews Avenue and Second Street.

West Palm Beach's store, at Clematis Street and Dixie Highway. "Sunshine Fashions" appeared prominently on both stores below the Burdine's name.

ATLANTIC *Truly Light* LUGGAGE

One of Burdine's most talked-about ads, in a vendor co-op sponsorship with Atlantic Luggage, featured three Miami icons: the gorgeous and quite famous Miami model Turalura Lipschitz (usually shown in ads with twin sister Tondalaya, but this ad required only one of the twins); a beautifully trained French poodle, Schlimiel, who loved posing for the ads; and, in the background, a Pan American World Airways double-decked Stratocruiser.

URDINE'S, FT. LAUDERDALE

goes Venetian . . . in honor of our beautiful city . . ."the Venice of America". . . we've created this elegant look in our lavish new dining room as well as our wonderful new world of fashion on the second floor. Venetian arts and imports will always have a special niche at Burdine's . . . their opulence and beauty are both a leading trend in fashion and home decor. Proudly we take another step forward in the magic growth of Ft. Lauderdale and South Florida.

Dining at Burdine's was meant to be a treat, and for many years, until the food services were deemphasized, each store had its own fine dining room. Shown here are the front and back of the Fort Lauderdale store's Venetian Room menu, the store featuring its own specially prepared sandwiches and salads along with hot entrées.

- The "Hilton" name was not added to the name of the hotel until it was taken out of bankruptcy in 1978 by a worthy successor to Novack's vile legacy, and that legal action was thirty-five years after the issue of the supposed newspaper was published;
- Finally, the LaRonde Room was the Fontainebleau Hotel's great showroom, the largest hotel showroom ever built on Miami Beach up until that time, and it was as new as the hotel was when it opened in 1954.

As noted, that is just one of the misstatements that could not have been found in any written material, as no such "facts" had ever been previously published. Rather, they had to have been fed to a person brought in from New York by the company to write its history, she knowing very little about the history of either Miami or the store, while those taking advantage of her had to have been quite versed in the history of both entities.

At any rate, George Whitten, after his many years of service to the company and as de facto head, was promoted in 1943 to the presidency, with William Burdine becoming chairman of the board. Horace Cordes, after fourteen years with the firm, was named executive vice-president and treasurer, while Freeland Cresap, following a devoted twenty-four years with the company, was named vice-president and secretary.

William, a great outdoorsman and sportsman, was essentially freed from his day-to-day responsibilities and, much to his happiness, was able to spend a great deal more time on his ranch. George Whitten, who started his career with Burdine's as a part-time summer employee and then spent his entire working life there, was as responsible for the growth and greatness of Burdine's as any member of the family. While the stores are now named "Macy's," and while many of them have changed locations one or more times, Whitten's name must always remain and be memorialized at the same level as William Sr., Roddey, Freeman and William Jr., for he had been with the firm in some capacity and grown with it for thirty-two years at the time he became president.

The horrors of World War II began to wind down beginning with the June 6, 1944 D-day landings on the Normandy beaches in France, and as each month passed, the anticipation of the coming end of the war became more palpable. People in Burdine's stores and in Greater Miami talked regularly about their futures following the war and began making plans for the aftermath.

Whitten, as company president, knew that much had and would continue to change, and he wanted to do whatever was necessary to prepare for a South Florida future in which Burdine's would play a major role. Beginning in late 1944, Whitten began what he referred to as "planning meetings" that were, in effect, brainstorming sessions directed toward thinking about how Burdine's would address its and the region's future—particularly thinking about what he strongly believed would be major population increases following the war and how they would affect Burdine's business.

In brainstorming, all comments are supposed to be welcomed, and participants are assured that nothing is off-limits or out of bounds, hence all were encouraged to add their thoughts to the discussions. While the idea of "suburban" stores such as Dadeland Mall, Westland Mall or even North Miami Beach's 163rd Street Shopping Center was well in the future, and the idea of becoming part of a national organization with a Federated or Allied Stores type of affiliation was not even within the bounds of one's imagination, what did arise from those meetings was the idea that given the time and the populations bases, just as Miami, Miami Beach and West Palm Beach had proven to be such "winners," so would a downtown Fort Lauderdale store. What had started as just some notes on scratch paper eventually evolved into, with its early 1950s opening, another of the chain's highly successful properties.

In August 1945, following the defeat of Germany three months earlier, Japan surrendered unconditionally, and with those victories, the troops began returning home shortly thereafter, to be greeted joyously by friends, families and loved ones. Burdine's, with its forward-looking thinking and with the preparations that it had made over the several months before the end of hostilities in Europe and the Far East, was well positioned to welcome the returning heroes home.

With mostly streamlined passenger trains of two different railroads serving two Miami depots (the FEC's just two and a half blocks from the main store on Flagler Street and Seaboard's about three miles from downtown at 2206 Northwest Seventh Avenue), as well as regular and reliable airline service with increasingly powerful propeller-driven planes, the immediate postwar boom was such that it appeared to rival what had happened in the 1920s. All three Burdine's stores instituted regular nighttime hours, and Thursday and Friday evenings downtown were regular nights out for dates or families. With the terrible memories of World War II slowly beginning to fade, it was time for management to prepare for what certainly lay ahead.

Resistance Is Futile

We know that nobody can predict the future, although with Miami's 50th birthday being celebrated the year after World War II ended, a pretty good effort was made by the city fathers to do just that. In 1946, the city published a soft-cover booklet detailing what its writers believed Miami would look like and be like in 1996, when it would celebrate, in concert with the FEC Railway, its 100th birthday. The booklet is revealing, fascinating and certainly futuristic.

Among the items in the booklet and predicted for the future included a permanent world's fair in Miami (attempts would be made to build something called "Interama," but that resulted, after a number of false starts, in abject failure); a great building near downtown with a roof large enough for airplanes to land on; a consolidated railroad station so that the FEC and the Seaboard would operate out of a "union" station; and much more. Some of the ideas and concepts proved viable and usable, while others were mere fantasy, but it certainly was fodder for discussion. Very few copies of that booklet exist today, and those that do are certainly Miami memorabilia treasures.

But what about the chapter title "Resistance Is Futile?" What does that mean, and how does it relate to the history of Burdine's? Simply put, "Resistance is futile" was the mantra of "the Borg," a race that traveled through space in a cube-shaped, planet-sized spaceship on the television show *Star Trek* and in the movies of the same name. They were so powerful that, after giving the three-word warning, they would simply absorb the people or beings on the planet that was their target.

The ten years from 1946 until 1956 were not, either in the history of Burdine's or the history of Federated Department Stores, a lifetime. But resistance to the merger, which was approved by Burdine's stockholders in May 1956 and became effective on July 28, 1956, Miami's sixtieth birthday, would have been futile indeed.

For better or for worse, Miami was changing following the war, and Burdine's had to change with it or be left behind. In 1946, three separate groups of "boat people" arrived on the shores of South Florida, but in what might be a shocking revelation to today's Miamians, they were not Cubans but rather a total of forty-seven Baltic refugees from Estonia who managed to survive their Atlantic crossings and arrive on Miami's shores between August 20 and September 28, 1946. All of them, because of the humanitarian efforts of Florida senator Claude Pepper, who urged President Harry Truman to allow them to stay, were given immigration papers on November 1, 1946. Eventually blending in with the community, they formed the Estonian-American Cultural Club in Hialeah, which apparently was still in existence in mid-1980, but given the changing times and the movement of the young people to different locales, it is no longer in operation.

A great deal was occurring in the Burdine's domain, and major strides were made in the ten years before the Federated merger to expand the company's size, name and reach. Plans that had been delayed due to the war years were dusted off. Work began in 1946 to expand the store to the corner of Flagler Street and Miami Avenue, the remaining portion of the old Biscayne Hotel being bulldozed and removed so that the store could be extended. At the same time, a basement for storage purposes was added, and a large stainless-steel overhead connecting bridge was put in place between the main store on the east side of Miami Avenue and the annex on the west side. That bridge, which connected the third, fourth and fifth floors of the two buildings, not only allowed customers access to both sides of the store without having to go outside (a great convenience in the muggy late springs, summers and early falls in Miami) but also provided the perfect location for the store's famous and enormous Santa Claus beginning just before Thanksgiving and lasting until just after New Year's Day.

By the time the work on the Miami store was completed, the street frontage on Flagler, Miami Avenue and Southeast First Street totaled about 1,100 feet.

An absolutely marvelous January 2, 1955 aerial photo shows us downtown Miami as it was a year and a half before Federated took over. The tallest building in the picture, just to right of center in the foreground, is the Dade County Courthouse. The curved building, lower right, is the old *Miami Herald* building, and Burdine's is just behind it on the far right of the photo, the nine-story tower sticking up in front of Richards and the Seybold Arcade. The FEC tracks are just to the left of the courthouse, and a Miami not yet ravaged by high rises stretches north from the camera.

On August 1, 1946, work began on the demolition of the old Fort Lauderdale City Hall and fire station at the corner of Andrews Avenue and south Second Street. According to the Fort Lauderdale Historical Society, the beautiful Mediterranean-style city hall had been designed by architect John Peterman, who was the first architect to open an office in that city and went on to design a few other buildings there, including several government buildings and schools. The new store was planned to have three stories (four if counting the balcony as an additional floor), as well as a service/storage area, and would extend 235 feet along Andrews, with a depth of 130 feet back to a service alley. It is not known for certain today if the storage/service area and parking garage were built in concert with the main building or added later. It does appear, in a color image contained in the Bramson

Archive, that the additional space may have been built after the construction of the store itself was completed and may not have been built as part of the original structure. With a grand ceremony, attended by numerous Fort Lauderdale and Broward County dignitaries and presided over by George Whitten and Fort Lauderdale's mayor, the store was opened in 1947.

Numerous changes in fashion followed the war, and Burdine's had no small part in accelerating them, becoming not only the style forerunner in terms of swimwear and resort wear but also a national force in bringing new styles in women's bathing attire to prominence. Women, even in the years leading up to World War II, were expected to be demure when they engaged in "surf bathing," but after the war, the styles lent themselves to more freedom for the ladies—the one-piece bathing suit became completely acceptable, followed not too many years later by the showings of the two-piece "bikini" bathing suit (covered, of course, when going to and from the beach or pool by the appropriate resort-oriented clothing), as well as highly attractive casual pants outfits.

With more and more tourists flocking to Miami Beach, Miami and resorts north to Palm Beach for the winter, the shops on Collins Avenue, Lincoln Road and Flagler Street were selling and arranging for the shipping of fresh Florida citrus anywhere in the country, generally by Railway Express Agency, utilizing fast passenger trains with their own dedicated Railway Express Agency refrigerator cars, which gave next-day delivery to New York and second-day delivery to Chicago and midwestern points. Noting that an entirely new opportunity was opening for them, the powers that were at Burdine's, several of whom lived on Miami Beach, recognized a unique opportunity for the department store chain.

Burdine's formed its own fruit shipping department, but contrary to what Ms. Morgan wrote—that "[d]uring the winter season of '46, Burdine's sale and shipment of tropical fruits became so important that the store began operating its own packing house"—there is no documentation to support such a comment. Rather, it appears that arrangements were made, similar to those made with the cosmetics companies for counter and display space in the various stores, for one or more lessees to operate, at least in the Miami, Fort Lauderdale and West Palm Beach stores, a fruit shipping department in which "tropical candies," usually coconut and chocolate specialties along with guava, mango and other jellies from fruits only available in the

The beautiful cover of the
downtown Miami store's
Hibiscus Tea Room menu
enclosed two pages of dining
delights for businessmen,
shoppers and tourists.

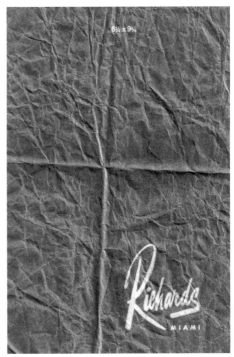

Incredibly, this small Richards shopping
bag has been preserved and is now in the
Bramson Archive. Until Jordan Marsh
opened, Richards was Burdine's only
true department store competitor.

tropics, as well as various mixed nuts sold with the Burdine's label, were available. (There was no fruit shipping department in the Miami Beach Lincoln Road store, although, when it first opened, there was a small fruit shipping department in the new Miami Beach store at Seventeenth Street and Meridian Avenue.)

The fruit shipping labels appeared with the name "Sunshine Fruits from Burdine's" on them, but it is highly unlikely that Burdine's would have had any interest in spending the money to either buy or take over and then operate its own packinghouse, which would have required even then a major outlay for one or more buildings, equipment, service facilities, loading docks and, of course, personnel. In addition, dedicated vehicles would have been required to bring the boxed product to the nearest Railway Express office. Obviously, it was easier and simpler for Burdine's to have arranged to have somebody else make up the displays, do the order taking, packaging and shipping and send out all products with a Burdine's private label on the packages and boxes.

It would be during that time that Burdine's began to reach out to the community in ways other than fashion shows, utilizing store facilities (particularly the new auditorium and the several meeting rooms) for business conferences, bridal shows and lectures on different topics ranging from use of kitchen utensils to color and fabric matching and on to preparing for and caring for newborns. A service was started whereby those wishing to purchase one or more rooms of furniture and furnishings could take advantage of Burdine's in-house decorators, and that proved very popular, increasing furniture and appliance sales.

Hurricanes, always something that South Floridians have been concerned with, were a different issue. With the new buildings, the store's management, similar to the thinking of the Miami Beach hotel owners during this decade, decided that in the event of or even the threat of a storm, they would need not only to be well prepared but also to afford employees food and shelter. Special facilities were prepared, and according to company records, the downtown Miami store provided food and housing for several hundred employees when a hurricane emergency was declared. It was still a very paternal organization.

During the following year, a number of departments were moved. Among the major changes, the furniture and appliance departments were moved into the west building. The coffee shop was also moved there and was located on the first floor, not only relieving the tearoom (the main dining room) of some of its traffic but also encouraging patrons who wanted to stop in for just a cup of coffee to be able to do so and not feel that they were taking up valuable table space that was supposed to be used for full meals. The coffee shop (the Burdine's Grill) was also open for breakfast beginning at 7:30 a.m., and the traffic was nonstop throughout the day. Like so many Miamians who spent some time as Burdine's employees, the author was assistant manager of the food division of the downtown store. More on that later, though.

Beginning August 1, 1948, the first of what later would prove to be several management restructurings would take place. All top management remained in the same positions and offices, but several formal committees were created, including finance, operations and management and community involvement. It was to the latter committee that the various store managers were able to present their ideas for being an integral part of the various cities and organizations that they felt would be important for the continued welfare of the store and its employees—not overlooking, of course, the importance of encouraging those organizations to patronize Burdine's to an even greater degree.

Through the community involvement committee, arrangements were made to pay for store manager's memberships in various service organizations such as Lions and Optimist Clubs, as well as others, and the store began to sponsor Little League baseball teams. Another area that was considered important was advertising in high school yearbooks, which at that time was not an overly expensive affair, considering that the entire tri-county area contained a total of eight public high schools, with five of those in Dade County, including Miami Beach, Miami Edison, Miami High, Miami Jackson and Redlands or Homestead High. The company's management recognized quite early that the young people, many of whom patronized Burdine's as teenagers, were certainly the next generation of dedicated customers.

In 1948, the chain celebrated, in all four of the stores, the company's fiftieth anniversary, and it was, particularly in downtown Miami, a bang-up affair. The one tiny emporium that had been overseen by William Burdine and son John had grown in those fifty years to a four-store giant, the largest retail store in South Florida.

Sears, Roebuck and Company had its store in Miami well north of downtown Biscayne Boulevard, and Saks Fifth Avenue had a Lincoln Road

The beautiful Lincoln Road and Meridian Avenue Miami Beach store. After Burdine's moved to the new store, two blocks north on Seventeenth Street and Meridian, the old store sat empty for several years until Richards took it over, remaining there until the chain was liquidated.

store on Miami Beach, and other than five-and-ten-type chain stores such as Woolworth's, W.T. Grant, Kresge, McCrory's and Kress, Burdine's only serious competition was Richards on Northeast First Avenue between First and Second Streets. To a lesser extent, there was Jackson's and Byron's, which were "second-level" department stores that in the late 1960s would merge under the combined name and then eventually drop the Byron's name and operate for a few more years as Jackson's before being purchased by Miami Beach hotelier Harry Mufson and becoming Jefferson Stores—that chain has now also disappeared from the Miami scene.

Richards began as the New York Department Store, and then the name was changed to reflect the ownership of the Cromer and Cassel families, they eventually being bought out by a New York firm that changed the name to the Mark Store; another sale changed the name again, this time to

Richards, the name that many Miamians still fondly remember. Eventually, Richards became part of another department store holding company, City Stores Corporation. While certainly a good store, Richards never reached the level of perception of quality that the Burdine's name evoked. In fact, for several years, one of Richards most famous ads noted, "We're Richards—and that's OK!" as if to tell the public that while it might not have been Burdine's, it still wasn't a bad place to shop. Until Allied Stores opened Jordan Marsh on Fifteenth Street and Biscayne Boulevard in 1956, though, Burdine's really had very little in the way of serious competition other than from neighborhood specialty stores such as those selling furniture and appliances. William Burdine's original competitors—Isidor Cohen, the Sewell brothers, E.B. Douglas, D.R. Knight, J.W. Harper and all the rest—had simply ceased to exist.

With the fiftieth anniversary at hand, the tiny wooden building of 1898 had grown to become a colossus, with more than $26 million dollars in annual sales. The 3,300 employees of the four stores were still treated like family, which is how George Whitten, having been taught by Roddey Burdine, wanted everybody to feel.

The employees were responsible for looking after not only the customers but also the operational needs of the four stores, and the personnel included not only direct, face-to-face customer sales clerks, fashion consultants, home decorating consultants and a growing dining room and grill serving staff but also a large number of behind-the-scenes employees whom customers likely never saw, including buyers and merchandise managers, air conditioning and refrigeration people, cleaning staff, equipment maintenance crews, credit management staff, human resources (then called the personnel department), vehicle maintenance staff, accounting staff and management people. By the early 1950s, Burdine's vehicle fleet was the largest privately owned automobile and truck fleet in the state—referring to retail, of course. Even the FEC Railway, which had not yet gone into piggybacking, had only three company vehicles assigned to the Miami station and Buena Vista Yard. Additionally, the stores had safety experts, now referred to as risk managers, whose jobs entailed doing everything possible at all times to keep the premises and work environment safe and free of hazards that might cause liability. They, additionally, were responsible for safety training, which all employees went through as part of their orientation following hiring.

Burdine's, by that time, had its own security director, who was equivalent to being chief of police in a small town, with both uniformed and plainclothes agents who were responsible not only for curtailing shoplifting (by both the public and employees) but also for keeping the property and premises secure, including attempting to prevent crimes against both property and customers—particularly the ever-present problem of pickpockets.

The third-floor main store beauty salon published this three-page brochure ballyhooing its services in the early 1950s. The phone number at the time was 3-1141.

Over the years, and because of both his education and the tutelage he had received from Roddey, George Whitten completely understood the importance to the stores of happy employees who felt that they were always treated fairly and with respect. Whitten, with his degree, was always open to the use of new management insights and techniques, and with that knowledge, he initiated such Burdine's hallmarks as pension and retirement plans, medical insurance, in-house employee recreation and relaxation facilities and, perhaps most importantly to many employees, generous discounts on all store purchases—ranging, depending on the items, from 15 percent and up. That, for many of the Burdine's staff, made a substantial difference.

George, who believed very strongly in both store and employee community involvement, quietly ordered in 1949 the world's largest, full-color, neon Santa Claus, and on Thanksgiving night in 1950, more than ten thousand Miamians and visitors jammed downtown Miami, crowding out all car and bus traffic on Flagler Street and North and South Miami Avenues in order to watch Santa being turned on for the first time, a tradition that would last into the early 1960s, when the cost of replacing the neon tubing and maintaining and storing the seventy-five-foot-tall figure had reached the point that an honorable retirement for the jolly gent was at hand. The *Miami Herald*, in a laudatory editorial, commended the store and its management on its contributions to the community, even though it lamented the end of the "yearly tradition that has brought so many smiles to so many Miamians."

Unfortunately, the years before and after World War II and up to and through the passage of the Civil Rights Act of 1964 were terrible years of segregation in Miami, as well as in the rest of the South. The year 1956 would bring the merger with Federated Department Stores. The northern interests—those Federated managers who came to Miami to begin the amalgamation process—were made to understand that, while many of the local employees and managers resented, disagreed with or disliked the fact that by Florida state law separate men's and ladies' rooms and separate water fountains had to be maintained (an annoying and expensive requirement), it was also one that, if not followed, could lead to the arrest of the store's managers for violating the state law.

Many Miamians clearly remember the signs on the streetcars (until 1940) and then the buses that noted that "Colored Seat From the Rear," and so it was in the four Burdine's stores, with signs over the water fountains that read

"Colored" or "White." Men's and ladies' rooms had signs specifying which race and which gender could use each facility. Even worse, black Miamians, who had always been allowed, if not encouraged, to shop at Burdine's, knew that they were forbidden from entering the tearoom or sitting at the counter in the grill. Although they could order food to take out from the grill's counter, they could not be seated in any of the store's food and beverage operations.

The same situation was present in the clothing departments. Black customers, including those from the Bahamas, could buy clothing, but they were not allowed to use the dressing rooms, requiring them to make their purchases without trying on what they were buying, a privilege white customers always expected and had. Moreover, blacks were not allowed to return any clothing items, so if a dress, a pair of slacks, a bathing suit or a jacket were flawed, it was immaterial.

Many people, such as the Bramsons, who came to Miami Beach from New York in 1946 found the "peculiar institution" known as segregation to be both distasteful and disturbing, knowing that it simply was not the right thing to do. It was the law, however, and beyond resenting it, there was little at the time that individuals of good conscience could do about it. At any rate, that was the situation in the South, not just in Miami or in Florida, in the years leading up to the merger.

By the 1950s, with an amazing record of growth, Greater Miami, as well as the rest of South Florida, had become a year-round resort, made possible, to no small extent, through the miracle of almost universal air conditioning. Capitalizing on the patronage of wealthy Latin American businessmen and tourists, the company initiated the first of its very popular mail-order catalogues, those printed in Spanish to serve customers in Central and South America. Those customers included American military personnel stationed in Cuba and Panama's Canal Zone, and every six months a supply ship was sent from Cuba to be loaded with material ordered from Burdine's, while a plane was sent from Panama on a regular schedule to do the same thing.

It was in the mid-1950s when the store developed its very popular and very competitive Teen Boards, which the company used to "consult with" youth on new young people's fashion trends and styles. Benefits of being a Burdine's Teen Board member included store ID badges, complimentary meals when asked to come to the store as part of a board function and clothing (that which members of the board tried on), as well as discounts on future purchases.

By 1950, sales in the four stores totaled $27.8 million, with a net profit of $1.1 million, but there were problems with the huge differential in seasonal business and the fact that, as a matter of location, sales declined tremendously from late spring until late fall. During the early 1950s, the company began experiencing financial difficulties with what analysts refer to today as "constricted cash flow."

In the winter, sales exploded, but summers could be very difficult, and several longtime Miamians shared with the author the fact that, in the first years of the 1950s, they, as year-round residents, would go shopping on Lincoln Road during the summer and find that the Miami Beach Burdine's store felt "empty"—the clerks basically stood around looking bored, and the number of customers on each floor was so few that they could be counted on one hand.

By November, although sales were beginning to slowly improve, and even with the knowledge that the improvement would increase over coming weeks and into "the season," the company's credit line was exhausted, and buyers were constrained from placing orders until after the first of the new year, when the Christmas shopping season had replenished the proverbial till. In the summer of 1954, Mr. Burdine and Mr. Whitten arranged to refinance the corporate debt through the instrument of a twenty-year $5.5 million loan, which was in addition to a sale and leaseback of the property on which the West Palm Beach store sat.

With all of that, Burdine's was not immune to competition. The lure of the "Magic City," with its delightful weather for most of the year, its ongoing growth and its future growth potential, led Allied Stores, the owners of the Jordan Marsh store brand, to consider the possibilities of a Miami location. Once the decision was made, Allied moved quickly to establish not just a foothold but a dedicated clientele for Jordan Marsh.

In 1955, Allied Stores Corporation purchased a large piece of property just north of the longtime favorite Miami dining spot, the Red Coach Grill. Fronting Biscayne Boulevard on the west and Northeast Fifteenth Street on the south, the projected building would cover much of the block on which the store would be built. That location was the site of a longtime Miami attraction, the beloved "pony track," the disappearance of which distressed a large number of Miami residents and their children. But progress would not be held back, and in 1956, with great fanfare and publicity, the new Jordan

Marsh store was opened with, among its many attractions, a lovely, bright and airy dining room called the Gulfstream Room, which immediately drew a large number of patrons who, frankly, were tired of the "same old menu" and "the same old food" in the Flagler Street Burdine's tearoom.

The Jordan Marsh store was an immediate success, and Allied, quick to capitalize on its first southern outlet, came up with slogans such as, "Florida's high fashion department store," and, "The store with the Florida flair." If Burdine's did not move quickly to regain the business, it knew that it would be in trouble. Almost from the beginning, "JM," as it came to be known, not only initiated many of the programs that Burdine's had begun years previously but also began a series of popular music concerts held on its east-side patio that drew large numbers of locals to the store. Whitten and his associates knew that they had their work cut out for them.

George Whitten and the Burdine's Board of Directors recognized the fact that, unquestionably, they would have no choice but to grow, but with limited funds for major expansion, they would also have no choice but to affiliate with an organization that had deep pockets even then. That organization was the Federated Department Store chain, and Burdine, Whitten and the board knew that they would either have to accept the inevitable change or be buried by the refusal to do so. Simply put, resistance would have been futile.

Expanding Throughout Florida

The situation worsened as competition from the new Jordan Marsh store diminished Burdine's prevailing market share. Jordan Marsh offered shoppers an elegant new browsing and shopping environment with a wonderful new restaurant, and that, combined with the buying power of the parent company, Allied Stores Corporation, allowed the store to stock a wider selection of merchandise. After several years of actually resisting Federated's offers to acquire the four-store Burdine's chain, the family, Mr. Whitten and the board finally accepted the Federated offer; a stock swap valued at $18.5 million completed Federated's subsuming of Burdine's in May 1956.

Shortly after Federated became the ownership entity of Burdine's, Alfred H. Daniels was named president, with Mr. Whitten becoming chairman of the board. Mr. Daniels, as it turned out, had one close relative in the Miami area, a first cousin. Anna (Mickey) Tobin's father was Daniels's mother's brother, and throughout their lives the families had kept in close touch. By a twist of good fortune, Myrna and the author were introduced to Mickey and her husband, Sherman, and became good friends, with Mickey mentioning Mr. Daniels and Burdine's on numerous occasions throughout the years of the friendship.

When I told Mickey that I was going to write the history of Burdine's, she became ebullient, for she and Sherman (he the 7 Up bottler in Greater

This page: The opening of Jordan Marsh, "The store with the Florida flair," was the first real and true challenge to Burdine's South Florida hegemony, as no other store had ever presented an array of offerings and goods at the level that Burdine's had. With "JM" coming to town, Burdine's was in for a major battle for the hearts, minds and wallets of Miamians. The original JM store, at Fifteenth Street and Biscayne Boulevard, opened with three stories and, within a short time, had added two additional floors.

Miami) had not only kept a written record of her cousin's achievements but also had been his closest friends and confidants during his years in Miami. The Tobins, as it turned out, not only socialized on a regular basis but also were invited, according to Mickey, to every Burdine's affair and event that was held during Alfred's tenure as Burdine's "boss."

While Burdine's, in the years following Mr. Daniels's retirement, would certainly have some fine top-level management, there was nobody quite like Al Daniels, and even during my stint as assistant manager of the food division of the downtown store, I would occasionally hear employees speak glowingly and wistfully of their years with him as president of the company—Alfred H. Daniels was truly beloved and was a man in the mold of Roddey Burdine and George Whitten.

Daniels was a native of Pittsburgh, but early in his life his parents moved to Rochester, New York, where his father opened a retail store. Alfred graduated from high school in Rochester, but incredibly enough, a Miami connection was already in play that early in Daniels's life, for his father and mother became friends with Mr. and Mrs. Harvey Baker Graves, who owned the largest furniture store in New York State between Albany and Buffalo.

Graves, in 1918, made his second trip to Florida and his first trip to Miami, and it was during that trip that he and several friends took an excursion via a launch up to the northern end of Biscayne Bay. It was on that little journey that Graves would "discover" the islands and beachfront that he would purchase from the Flagler System shortly thereafter and name them "Sunny Isles," today's beautiful city of Sunny Isles Beach. In addition, he purchased mainland property, and although he never developed it, he did donate about fifty-five acres to Dade County, a tract that is now called East Greynolds Park.

Having graduated from Harvard magna cum laude and as a member of Phi Beta Kappa in 1933, young Alfred had planned to study law. Unfortunately, with the Depression at hand, and with his family having lost its modest wealth because of the financial downturn, he decided instead that he would go for a graduate business degree. He was accepted at Harvard's business school and graduated with an MBA in 1935.

His first job following graduation was at *Vanity Fair*, but with business conditions as they were, the publication soon folded. On the flip of a coin in 1936, he passed up a job at Lehman Brothers, the famous financial institution and brokerage house, and chose Federated Department Stores. He went on to a long and distinguished career with Federated, and in 1971 he moved to San Francisco to become the CEO of the chain's famed I. Magnin stores on the West Coast.

Mickey Tobin recalls her and her husband's time with Daniels while he was in Miami, beginning late in 1956. "Naturally," Mickey said, "the announcement of my cousin Alfred's becoming president of Burdine's was very exciting news as we had seen him regularly over the past several years while he was working in New York and vacationing in Miami, and when he told us that he would be moving here and taking the position of Burdine's president, we were thrilled." (Daniels was with Abraham & Strauss in New York for twenty years before his coming to Miami as president of Burdine's.)

As the South Florida 7 Up bottler, Sherman Tobin was very well connected and was a member not only of several yacht and social clubs but also, perhaps more importantly, of the prestigious Westview Country Club. One of the first things that Sherman did upon Alfred's taking up residency in Miami was to shepherd him through the nomination and acceptance process of Westview membership, which placed him in good stead during his years in Miami.

Not only was the tearoom at the main store a favored place for the ladies, its Men's Grill was the downtown Miami dining spot of choice for executives long before there were dining clubs in the city.

In 1959, having learned of Burdine's marvelous history, Daniels decided that he wanted to do something special to commemorate the store's sixty-one years of existence: to "throw a little party for the whole town." That party was meant to be a re-creation of Burdine's origins, as well as to celebrate the store's history and the growth of the city. A replica of the very first store was constructed inside the Flagler Street store, and many of Miami's and Fort Lauderdale's pioneers participated by loaning memorabilia, as did the Seminole and Miccosukee Indian tribes. A flyer was printed up and distributed, and following a brief history of the store, the flyer, in referring to Burdine's belief in treating its customers fairly, noted: "Later, about sale items, he [William Burdine] advertised: 'We have them ojus and no humbug. We make no claim to sell goods at cost all the time, but when we announce a special bargain sale, it means something. And it still does!'"

The main store lunch counter in the 1940s, later given more space and moved to the southwest side of the new building on the west side of Miami Avenue.

The flyer continued:

There is little specific information about Burdine's first store. The section which you see re-created during this 1959 Anniversary Sale is the product of reminiscences of a lot of fine people whose families or research have given them a good notion of what it was like. Burdine's is grateful to Mrs. Sydney Weintraub, whose father opened a store in 1896 [Clare Cohen Weintraub was the daughter of Ida and Isidor Cohen, and she was the first Jewish baby born in Miami]; *to Mrs. Frank Stranahan, whose husband ran a store in Fort Lauderdale long before that; to Fae Cunningham, John Sherman and others of the Miami Pioneers; Earnest Gearhart of the Historical Association of Southern Florida; Julia F. Morton and Helen Muir, who have a rare knowledge of our city; Mrs. E. Hugh Duffy (daughter of famed captain Charlie Thompson); to Jane Wood, Lep Adams, Henry Shaw, Roy Perry, Wirth Munroe, Arthur Griffith, who lent exhibits; and to the independent nations of the Miccosukees and Seminoles tribes, which held conferences to ask their elders to recall their shopping days at the first Burdine's, and thanks to Jimmy Tiger, Bobby Tiger, Tiger Tiger, William McKinley Osceola and Smallpox Tommy.*

The Brooklyn Museum lent precious articles from their costume collection which is the largest in the world. The White Sewing Machine Co. sent their 1890s model; see Warner's corsets of the '90s. Butterick Printed Patterns were not printed in 1898 or even sold in envelopes but the tissue patterns of the day are here on loan from the president's private collection. Coast & Clark were the dominant thread company; LaMode Buttons have been stylish since '77; Loewenthal Trimmings were in a heyday. Lamps come from the White Elephant Shop, Margate, and many an idea from Smallwood's Store, Chokoloskee.

Below that copy, in large letters, is printed "GREAT ATTRACTIONS!" under which are the words, "Dainty Calicos, Genuine Bandannas, Horehound and Cut Rock Candy. Buy Yours at Old-Time Prices. Burdine's 1898 Store, Second Floor [Miami]."

Although some readers may note apparent misspellings or words that seem out of place or out of context ("see Warner's corsets of the '90s"), nothing has been changed, and the wording above has been taken exactly and directly

This page: The Dadeland Store was not just huge; it was, for many years, not only the largest suburban department store in America but also the number one grossing suburban department store in the country. These two views will give the reader an idea of the immensity of the building.

from the 1959 flyer. Sadly, and to the best of our knowledge, not a single person listed in the flyer is alive today, and equally unhappily, Burdine's never repeated that wonderful and historic event. Imagine what it could have and would have been like if the Bramson Archive was available then.

Alfred constantly brought new ideas and new thinking to Burdine's while maintaining the traditions of a great store. He was the consummate gentleman, and he would never allow rudeness or inappropriate behavior. Above all, he wanted the employees of the stores to know that his door was open to them at any time. Mary-Jo Horton, who joined the company in 1954 and later, in 1976, became its first female vice-president, was a great admirer of Daniels, and she was quoted in a 1960 *Women's Wear Daily* article on Daniels and his work for both Federated and Burdine's: "Federated could not have selected a finer gentleman for us than Al Daniels. We were all so pleasantly surprised."

George Whitten's mid-July retirement as Burdine's chairman (announced at a company seniority dinner on May 6, 1961, effective July 31, after forty-eight years with one company) was, while not unexpected, an unhappy moment for many longtime Burdiners who, in effect, had grown up with Mr. Whitten. But he knew that the time had come, and he left the company in excellent hands, Daniels being named a Federated vice-president, as well as Burdine's CEO, shortly after Whitten's retirement.

Daniels had been very disturbed with the segregation situation, and in 1961, after consulting with Federated's top brass in Cincinnati, Daniels announced that beginning on "the first working day of 1962 we will no longer refuse service to black patrons in the dining facilities of the Miami and Miami Beach stores." Fort Lauderdale and West Palm Beach were not included in the announcement, as apparently, the clientele in those two areas was not yet ready to accept integrated facilities.

On May 26, 1965, Daniels was named chairman and CEO of Burdine's, with Thomas Wasmuth, a thirty-year veteran of Rike's (headquartered in Dayton, Ohio), being named president. Together they oversaw Burdine's incredible growth.

Mickey and Sherman Tobin—who were invited to the opening of the new Westland store in Hialeah on what was then called Palm Springs Mile, today's West 49th Street in Hialeah, and Northwest 103rd Street in Miami-Dade County by her cousin, Alfred Daniels—recall that October 2, 1967 opening very well. "How could I not," Mickey says, smiling, "it was absolutely pouring that morning!" But even with that rough start, the Hialeah High School band played welcoming tunes, and Miss Hialeah cut the ceremonial ribbon. The sun immediately broke through the clouds, and the rest of the day was a typical and delightful early South Florida fall day.

Hialeah's mayor, Henry Milander, welcomed the Burdine's family and introduced the store's manager, George Corrigan, as well as "the fellow who is going to be George's assistant here in Hialeah, Burdine's Chairman of the Board Alfred H. Daniels." The crowd roared, and even though that glorious day is now more than forty-four years in the past, the warm memories still linger.

Later that month, though, Burdine's and the retail world would be shocked by the announcement of Alfred Daniels's retirement, to be effective on February 5, 1968, after thirty-one great years with the Federated chain. Tom Wasmuth would become chairman and CEO, and Al Daniels, after just a couple of months off, was asked to lecture at Columbia University, Harvard's Business School and Rochester Institute of Technology. In 1971, after telling Mickey and Sherman that "I really do miss the business," he became CEO of Federated's I. Magnin Division and was credited with toning down the store's snobbish image and broadening its appeal by enlivening the decor, adding less expensive clothing and encouraging clerks to be friendlier. He retired in finality in 1973 but still kept in occasional touch with the Tobins. On April 12, 1996, Alfred Daniels died in San Francisco, and Mickey Tobin said that she felt the same pain that she had when her brother died. "We loved him dearly, and he was a truly wonderful man," she told the author.

The second-largest department store group after Allied, Federated provided capital investment that significantly improved the merchandise mix at Burdine's and enabled the company to expand with new stores. Operating in one of the fastest-growing areas in the nation during the 1960s and 1970s, Federated planned two new Burdine's department stores with growth projections in mind and also after having done an extensive demographic study for each store. One of the two new stores was placed in Hialeah, northwest of Miami and close to a four-lane road that was built, at the time, "way out in the palmettos" north and west of the metro area. That road later became the never-ending traffic nightmare known as the Palmetto Expressway, with four lanes of twenty-four-hour-a-day traffic in each direction.

The Burdine's fruit labels were so popular that the store had them made into drink coasters.

In the case of the Kendall store, the company took somewhat of a chance, as it had with the Hialeah store, in regard to the idea of opening a large store in "far southwest Dade County." But to help ensure the store's success at the two locations, Burdine's acquired one-hundred- to two-hundred-acre parcels of land (another source shows the land purchases at about half that acreage, but half that acreage would not have permitted the very large shopping centers of which Burdine's was the main anchor) and sold the land surrounding the stores to mall developers. Thus, the two stores eventually became part of major shopping centers, specifically Westland

Mall and Dadeland Mall, and residential development followed commercial development. In 1971, the Dadeland Mall store became the largest-volume suburban department store in the country south of New York City.

Burdine's, with Federated's backing, then began a strong expansion throughout the state of Florida, initially in the Greater Miami area. During the late 1970s, the company expanded outside of southeast Florida for the first time. New stores were opened in Orlando and the Tampa Bay area, the latter including Sarasota, St. Petersburg, Clearwater and Tampa. New stores opened during the early 1980s included locations in Daytona Beach and Gainesville, followed by stores in Fort Meyers in southwest Florida and Melbourne along the central Atlantic coast. Locations relatively close to Miami in southeast Florida included Boca Raton, Hollywood and Cutler Ridge, below Dadeland farther south in Dade County. In 1984, Burdines Inc. opened a specialty store at the fashionable Shops of Mayfair in Miami's Coconut Grove neighborhood, selling men's and women's fashions and accessories, cosmetics and consumer electronics. The Mayfair store was never really successful, and in 1991, after seven frustrating years of working diligently to increase sales, the company made the difficult decision to close the store that, although located in an affluent area and in a unique shopping venue, never developed the level of revenue necessary to make it a success.

Between 1977 and 1985, Burdines Inc. expanded its chain from fourteen stores to twenty-nine stores, ranging in size from 50,000 square feet to more than 200,000 square feet. In 1985, sales reached $757.5 million.

Burdines Inc. refined its image as it grew during the 1970s and 1980s. As population growth in Florida attracted other department store chains to the state, Burdines Inc. developed "the Florida Strategy" to differentiate the company from the competition. Identified as "the Florida Store," the company highlighted the unique product offerings attributable to its experience and knowledge of Florida's tropical climate. When competing department stores from northern states offered dark colors and winter clothing, Burdine's stocked merchandise suitable to Florida weather. Winter merchandise included shorts, bathing suits, cotton sweaters and linen clothing but few winter coats.

Burdine's attention to demographics also extended to the needs of individual stores. Buyers selected merchandise in styles appropriate to the Palm Beach socialite or the midwesterner living on the Gulf Coast, depending on the location of the store. Burdine's provided an extended line of junior clothing for college students in the Gainesville area and petite-sized clothing for the Hispanic customers and Latin American tourists at the Dadeland store. As hip-hop style clothing became popular in the 1990s, the North Miami Beach store served the African American community with designer clothing from Karl Kani.

Burdines Inc. designed store interiors to fit the tropical atmosphere of Florida, as well as the location of the store. Designer Kenneth Walker applied tropical hues such as coral, turquoise and white, as well as beachside motifs such as the ocean, dolphins and palm trees. In Gainesville, home of the University of Florida, columns around the escalators resembled the school's alligator mascot. The Mayfair store, for its relatively short-lived tenure in upscale Coconut Grove, exuded elegance, with mirrored ceilings, marble flooring and columns in lacquered pastel colors. The stores featured atriums and skylights or ceilings painted sky blue with clouds. Plaster palm trees became informal trademarks of the company's identity as "the Florida Store." Officials at the company considered expanding to nearby states or to Puerto Rico during that time but ultimately decided to limit expansion to Florida so as not to dilute the Burdine's brand identity.

In 1986, the Campeau Corporation acquired the Allied Stores chain, followed in 1988 by its taking over of Federated through what was called a "leveraged" buyout, whereby it would sell off parts of the acquisition to pay most of the total purchase price, a financial gambit that began with the merger and acquisition firm of Kohlberg-Kravis-Roberts and was, on occasion, successful. It was not for Campeau, however, and the Canadian-based company, unable to meet its debt obligations, entered Chapter 11 Bankruptcy. It was during the course of the bankruptcy that Allied and Federated were merged into one company, with the Federated name surviving.

Federated closed four stores and sold seventeen stores, mostly Jordan Marsh and Maas Brother stores previously owned by Allied. This eliminated stores with low profits, as well as direct competition, as most stores were sold to mid-range department store chains such as Mervyn's, Montgomery Ward and J.C. Penney. Another seventeen Jordan Marsh and Maas Brothers stores were merged with Burdine's. When Federated emerged from bankruptcy, Burdine's thrived as a streamlined company of forty-four stores, with profit

The jewelry department at Burdine's was the equal of Miami's finest independent jewelry stores, and Burdine's had the advantage of co-branding, with manufacturers paying a sizable portion of the advertising cost, as was the case with Coro and its white jewelry as the most important accessory for resort wear.

margins at 12 percent, compared to 8 percent in 1986. Sales had declined under Campeau's ownership, attributed to lower-quality, lower-priced merchandise meant to stimulate cash flow through high sales turnover, but in 1991, following the merger and bankruptcy reorganization, Burdine's took over all of the former Allied Stores Tampa-based Maas Brothers/Jordan Marsh Florida division outlets, converting many to Burdine's and closing the rest. Burdines Inc. proceeded to revamp its product offerings, and in 1992, sales surpassed $1 billion for the first time, with fifty-eight Burdine's stores in the Sunshine State. The Dadeland store alone produced a bottom line net income of $30 million in profits.

Burdine's corporate attention thereafter returned to growth and expansion during the early 1990s. A new department store was opened in Pembroke Pines in 1992, and the company launched a new store concept, Burdine's Home Gallery, with those stores offering furniture, home accessories, fine china, silverware, glassware, housewares, electronics, gifts and floor coverings. In addition to small home stores, the company in November 1993 opened a 215,000-square-foot home furnishings store in the building once occupied by Jordan Marsh at Dadeland Mall. Home merchandise was relocated from the Burdine's department store at Dadeland to the Home Gallery, allowing the department store to double its clothing line. Burdine's then added significantly to the home furnishings line to fill the large new store.

The Burdine's Home Gallery offered an extensive line of high-quality home merchandise on three floors. The glassware selection featured crystal designed by Gianni Versace and Paloma Picasso, and the store dedicated an entire room to Waterford crystal. Electronics included the Oster line of 1950s retro-style kitchen appliances, and Burdines Inc. vigorously promoted the Home Gallery through sixty full-page advertisements in certain regional editions of the *Miami Herald*, on television, on billboards and in certain local magazines and business newspapers. Direct mail advertising to Burdine's charge card customers involved a forty-four-page catalogue, while the store's bridal registry alone required a staff of fifteen.

In 1994, Federated purchased Macy's Department Stores, raising questions about the possibility of changing Burdine's to the Macy's brand. In May 1996, Federated issued catalogues that were essentially the same, since both chains offered much of the same merchandise. Federated saved the expense of advertising by offering the same catalogue with the different brand names on the cover.

Burdine's became Federated's single most profitable division during the 1990s, even more profitable than Macy's and Bloomingdale's. Questions about a possible name change faded, at least for the time being, as Burdine's continued to expand with the moniker "the Florida Store" being added to the "Sunshine Fashions" byline.

To the great surprise, shock and unhappiness of almost every longtime Miamian, as well as most Miami historians, Burdine's participation in the FEC Railway and Miami Centennial event ranged from indifferent to nil. The event began in August 1995 and culminated with the bringing of the Florida East Coast Railway train to downtown Miami, complete with its historic display car for the weekend, ending on Sunday, July 28, 1996, the city's 100th anniversary; the event attracted more than 100,000 visitors. The chain's total contribution to the event, for which it did more during its sixty-first anniversary in 1959, was almost nothing as well.

Somehow, its decision of what to do for the centennial and its choice of how it would "participate" was quirky, if not bizarre: the great and historic Miami name, the longest-lived retailer under the same name in Miami's history, chose to have whales or dolphins in water (supposed to be the ocean?) painted on the east side of the downtown store. And that was it. Period. The store's nonparticipation was a bitter disappointment, and as America's senior collector of Miami memorabilia and Floridiana, I truly believe that the only word that can really be used is "shameful."

In 1998, the store "celebrated" its own centennial, and those who thought or believed that the owners were going to make up for the debacle of the lack of participation in the FEC Railway–City of Miami centennial were, again, hideously disappointed. To the best of any Miami historian's or collector's knowledge, there were only two things done for the company's own 100th anniversary: it sold custom-made Homer Laughlin Company Fiestaware pitchers, which held 67.5 ounces of liquid and stood seven inches tall, and it issued, either for sale or for gratuitous dispersal, a one-pint coffee mug with the same scene on the cup that had been painted on the store two years before.

To add insult to injury, the cup, around the top, has the words, "In Love with Florida for 100 Years," and in two places on the front of the cup, toward the bottom, are "100" over "Burdine's" over "Florida," with the word "Years" in tiny, barely readable print in the right side zero in the "100." There is also, just to the right of the handle, the following miniscule legend: "In celebration of Burdine's 100th anniversary. The Wyland Whaling Wall #78 'Florida's Ocean Life.'" And that was it. Burdine's entering of the new millennium came with a whisper, certainly not with a bang, at least as far as the celebration of its own history went. I am certain that all of the great names in the company's past, from William to Roddey, Freeman Burdine, George Whitten, Alfred Daniels and all the rest who cared about Burdine's history and tradition, were turning over in their respective graves.

In 1999 and 2000, the lack of respect for its own history notwithstanding, Burdine's experienced major growth, with seven new locations and major renovations of its existing stores. The new stores were unique, with more in the way of lighter colors and upgraded decor. The most anticipated of the new stores were at the Florida Mall in Orlando, Aventura Mall in Aventura (northeast Miami-Dade County, north of Miami), Citrus Park Town Center in Tampa, Oviedo Marketplace in Oviedo (a suburb of Orlando) and the Mall at Wellington Green in Wellington (a suburb of West Palm Beach), which opened in 2001.

The Aventura store, located almost in the physical center of the Aventura Mall, was a major facility and contained 226,000 square feet of retail space. Burdines Inc. promoted the store with an elaborate local transit bus advertising campaign: the fully painted exteriors of thirty-three public buses that stopped at Aventura Mall featured cooperative product advertising with Liz Claiborne, Ralph Lauren and other designer brands.

Burdine's then tried another new layout to test a new method designed to increase checkout convenience at St. Petersburg's Tyrone Square Mall. The store used a central checkout system that was expected to be more popular among shoppers since they would only need a cashier once before leaving. The design failed, however, since an employee had to manually apply a coded sticker (identifying who made the sale) to the price tag of each item before customers left the store. Burdine's quickly abandoned this plan and resumed its traditional cashier layouts.

The Dadeland Mall store, as mentioned, was not only the number one grossing suburban department store in the country south of New York, but with its 640,000 square feet of retail space in two buildings, including the Burdine's Home Gallery, the Dadeland Burdine's was also the largest suburban department store in the country.

In 2001, Burdine's initiated store renovations that established a sophisticated, contemporary look to reflect the international, refined taste of the company's customer base while maintaining the store's Florida identity. Burdine's began with the store at Aventura Mall. The company's identifying palm trees were recomposed in cast resin for a more elegant look. Tile flooring was custom-designed, with embedded seashells and sparkling flecks of mica. New lighting and sculptured palm trees on either side of the main entrance enhanced the store's exterior.

With the opening of its eighth furniture gallery, in Clearwater in 2001, Burdine's applied unusual merchandising techniques, as the store featured more home accents to create drama and glamour. For instance, a wall of Natuzzi chairs highlighted leather covers in bright colors. The floor plan combined with merchandise displays to lead customers to various sections of

This page: What Burdine's meant to Miami and the East Coast, Maas Brothers meant to the Tampa Bay area. Somewhat older than Burdine's, Maas Brothers was founded by Abe and Isaac Maas in 1886, growing from one small twenty-three- by ninety-foot store to a chain of thirty-nine stores across central and west coast Florida. The Maas Brothers name disappeared in 1991 when it was consolidated into Burdine's. Shown here are an early view of the downtown Tampa store and a very late 1940s view of the St. Petersburg store.

the store, where they encountered different styles and moods. The company applied these techniques at existing stores, as well as at the Fort Lauderdale Furniture Gallery, which opened in July 2002.

Burdine's remodeled stores in Hialeah, Miami and Orlando in 2002, and the company authorized a $50 million renovation of the Dadeland store as well, to occur in phases over three years. Improvements at Dadeland included the addition of a parking garage at the front of the store, wider aisles for ease of movement while shopping, a babysitting area and a day spa.

As the national economy slowed, Burdine's experienced a decline in sales, prompting the company to initiate several programs to attract customers. Burdine's sought to bring in young women by stocking hip styles in junior clothing and remodeling fitting rooms for comfort, with more space and the addition of lounge chairs. As discount mass merchandisers, such as Walmart and Target, began to sell clothing in fashion-forward styles, parent Federated suggested several strategies to compete with the discount chains. At two test stores, Burdine's provided shopping carts and price-check scanners and moved cash registers from each department to a central checkout area near the store exits.

Customers at the test stores did not like the new system, however, and complained—some loudly and vociferously—that it was more difficult to find a sales clerk to assist them in store departments; Burdine's halted the test program after five months and sought new ways to improve on service, including, among other innovations, testing the use of Palm Pilots in the shoe department. A sales clerk could check stock and request an item to be brought to the customer by a stock clerk without the sales clerk having to leave the customer.

With all of that, and with the growth, the profits, the innovations and the national and international recognition, the end was nigh. Beginning the following year, in 2003, the Burdine's name would start to fade, taking only a little more than two years to disappear from Miami's, and Florida's, history entirely.

The Name Disappears but the Memories Live On

In 2003, the top people at Federated made a series of significant decisions that would denude all of their regional affiliates of their names, no matter how meaningful those names were to the communities that they had been a part of for, in many cases, well over a century.

Federated actually originated in 1851, when the F&R Lazarus men's clothing store was founded by Fred Lazarus. Seventy-eight years later, in 1929, with Lazarus the major department store in Cincinnati, Federated Department stores was launched as a holding company for F&R Lazarus, Shillito's and Abraham & Strauss department stores. The following year, Bloomingdale's became part of the Federated group. Through the Depression years and into World War II, the group continued to expand, eventually subsuming Burdine's in 1956. In 1976, the group made a pivotal acquisition when the purchase of Rich's Inc. gave it a foothold in the Deep South retail business. The $157 million stock swap gave Federated control of the 109-year-old, Atlanta-based institution, with its eleven department stores, three Rich's II boutiques and eleven Richway discount stores in Atlanta, Birmingham, Alabama and Charlotte, North Carolina. From that base, Federated hoped to expand its operations throughout the remainder of the South.

Resistance was again futile, and the chain became a giant in American retailing second only to the Allied Stores group. In the early 1990s, the

GREAT ONCE-A-YEAR SALE OF FAMOUS

A. M. C. SHIRTS WITH IMPROVED

PERMASET TRUBENIZED COLLAR

•

ALWAYS AMERICA'S FINEST SHIRT VALUE

AT THE REGULAR PRICE OF $2.00

•

NOW!!!   FOR SHORT TIME ONLY—

$1.69

3 for $4.95

Burdine's is now but a memory, and that memory of wonderful days, wonderful times and wonderful prices lives on, an example being this store ad for AMC shirts, affordable for everybody at $1.69 each or three for $4.95.

decision was made to wipe out the Rich's name, and all of the stores of that former brand became Macy's. In 2003, as part of a plan to consolidate its holdings, parent Federated announced plans to begin converting the Burdine's name to that of Macy's, and on January 30, 2004, the fifty-six Burdine's stores were renamed Burdine's-Macy's, while, interestingly enough, the seven Macy's stores in Florida also became Burdine's-Macy's. Only a year later, on March 6, 2005, most of the regional names, including Burdine's but with the exception of the legendary Bloomingdale's, were dropped altogether. Within a very short time, all of the various stores' signs carried only the Macy's name, with only Marshall Field & Company in Chicago and its suburbs surviving under that revered name for another two years.

Obviously, with Burdine's and Macy's stores operating separately in several malls, consolidation was the next step, and as soon as was practicable, leases were cancelled and the operations consolidated into one store, Miami's Aventura Mall being an example.

There are very few American competitors remaining. Whether Saks Fifth Avenue, Dillards, the May Department Stores, Bonwit Teller, Lord & Taylor, Dayton-Hudson, Neiman Marcus or Nordstrom will fall prey to Federated is only a matter of conjecture, and only time will tell. In the meantime, Burdine's will live on, at least in the hearts, minds, memorabilia and images of so many people whose lives were touched by a once great company.

In preparing this book, the author reached out to numerous individuals for their recollections and remembrances of their time and experiences at Burdine's and found that the response was nothing short of massive.

Unfortunately, space limitations preclude the inclusion of more than a few, but those few, of employees (including this writer) and of "just folks," are meaningful and heartwarming. Typical among them are the memories of Roberta Small, who, with her degree in psychology, is a mental health counselor working for the State of Florida. Roberta remembers that trips to Burdine's, whether downtown or to the Miami Beach store, were times of great happiness, and her memories of going through the clothing racks and the shoe samples are, with her dear mother's warm smiles, still strong.

Even the packaging was both special and personal, as this made-for-Burdine's Control Top pantyhose box indicates. *Courtesy David Batista.*

Saralyn Nemser and her brother, Benjamin, have fond memories, particularly of the anticipation of going to downtown Miami on a Saturday with their mother and seeing the women wearing hats and white gloves. Saralyn's and Ben's mom, Myrna, actually has sharp memories of the famous snow princesses and snow clowns served to the children in the dining room. What a wonderful dessert that was! The snow princesses and the clowns were ice cream treats that came out with a china snow princess or a clown placed to appear as if it was the head on a princess's or clown's body, and there was whipped cream covered with silver sprinkles or "dots" that gave the princess or the clown its "clothing." Indeed, so many of Miami's children loved going to Burdine's so that they could have lunch in the tearoom and enjoy the snow princess or the clown as their dessert.

Barbara (Kaplan) Gertner graduated from Sophie Newcomb College of Tulane University in New Orleans, and while she was offered a position by a major New Orleans department store, she had always wanted to live in Miami. Although being a southern girl from Macon, her family had visited and stayed on Miami Beach numerous times. Her father, lovingly referred to as "Big Pa," was in the furniture business in Macon, and Barbara enjoyed going to his store and even working with the salespeople. Upon graduation in 1973, she was recruited by Burdine's as assistant furniture buyer for the chain.

Barbara's memories of her training and the time taken to prepare her for her position have never been forgotten, but to add to the happy memories, she has related to the author that as a college student she never drank coffee. And what is the significance of that? It seems that, every day, the buyers and their assistants took a coffee break, and as Barbara said, "What was I going to do? I never drank coffee in my life and suddenly there I was at 'coffee break,' so I drank coffee, and that became one of the most enjoyable parts of an always interesting day."

Shortly after arriving in Miami, and following orientation and training, Barbara was instructed to go out to the huge Burdine's warehouse at 7100 Northwest Thirty-second Avenue. Being from Macon and having spent four years in "Nawlins," even though she had vacationed years before on Miami

Susan Carrey was the youngest buyer and merchandise manager in Burdine's (and Federated's) history. A lovely and elegant lady then and now, Susan is shown at left with Burdine's personnel officer Andrea Edelstein on a buying trip to Italy in 1966. *Courtesy Susan Carrey.*

Beach, she had no knowledge of Miami's streets and avenues. Driving around aimlessly and completely lost, she finally wound up on Northwest Thirty-second Street and Seventy-first Avenue, as she said, "way, way, waaaaaay across town!" Eventually, she made it to the warehouse, but the story of the day she got lost in Miami on Burdine's business remains one of her great memories.

Another of the former Burdine's employees/associates who shared so much with me for this book was Susan Carrey, a twelve-year veteran of the company, being there from 1962 to 1974. Susan, at the age of twenty-two, became the youngest buyer in Burdine's or Federated's history and, at twenty-seven, became the youngest merchandise manager in both company's histories. Her mentor, who she warmly credits with much of her success (Susan would go on to a vice-presidency in an import apparel firm), was Joseph Brooks, another of the great names in Burdine's 1950s and 1960s history—he went on to become president of Lord & Taylor.

As author, it is my privilege and pleasure to relate several interesting events and incidences during my six months as assistant manager of the food division of the downtown store. Even though I was a graduate of the famed and renowned School of Hotel Administration at Cornell University, I was not, at that time, a "foodie," and in fact, I did everything that I could to avoid food-and-beverage-related courses, taking only the minimum required. Naturally, as fate has its way of doing, I spent the great majority of my career in the restaurant and club business, managing fine and high-grade operations, including the New York Gaslight Club and the Playboy Club Miami, with a five-year stint as catering director at Miami Beach's famous Epicure Market, all of that before I started teaching at the college level.

At any rate, upon graduation, I accepted an offer with a small hotel chain and worked in Dallas and Atlanta. Then I returned to Miami to become executive assistant manager of the Newport Motel. No food and beverage for me! After about two years at the hotel, I was offered a very exciting (so I thought) job as a district sales manager for the military division of the American Distilling Company. The company, however, was quite small and had only one or two known brand names, hence selling its products was anything but easy, so when the opportunity came to join Burdine's as assistant manager of the food division of the downtown store, I jumped at the opportunity. Food and beverage!? I had a Cornell degree, and I could do anything!

Without going into too many details, I still have some not-so-good memories of taking inventory on the last day of every month and having to put on the arctic coat to spend about an hour and a half in the walk-in freezer, then getting a cold within two days from the exposure to the icy air. We had two cooks who were terrific guys and who spent a good bit of time teaching me about the business. One of the men was "Smitty," and the other was a wonderful and most gracious black man by the name of "Sam," although regretfully, I never knew his last name. Some of the waitresses were real characters, and I do remember Betty and Ellen, whose nickname was "Tiger"—and she was!

Few things were as exciting as going to Burdine's for new clothes—even for the boys! Sally Bramson, to celebrate younger son Bennett's graduation from park school at Miami Beach's Stillwater Park, photographed him at the age of five in his brand-new, complete Burdine's outfit, the sport jacket finished with a handkerchief in the front pocket.

One of the greatest people I have ever worked with, before or since, was the woman who managed the coffee shop on the first floor in the west building. Blanche Stepanian was as knowledgeable as anyone I have ever known about coffee shop management and operation, and I enjoyed spending half an hour a day with her, having coffee and learning from her. I probably would have enjoyed being a Burdiner (loved the employee discounts!) to a much greater degree, but the manager of the division was an extremely difficult person to work for. After I left the company to become manager of a magnificent restaurant on Miami Beach called Lloyd's of the Maison Grande, my former boss at Burdine's became the food division manager for the entire chain but, within just a few years, was terminated by the company. Simply put, it was a blessing for me to have had the opportunity to have worked for Burdine's, to have had so many knowledgeable, caring and dedicated people as my co-workers and to have learned so much from them and from the company's policies.

The story of Burdine's just might have ended there but for a fortuitous (and accidental) meeting that occurred on Saturday night, August 27, 2011 in Stadnik's Drug Store in Miami Springs, the city founded by the great and famous American aviator, Glenn Curtis. With the city celebrating its eighty-fifth anniversary, the Stadniks decided to feature two scoops of ice cream for eighty-five cents at their luncheonette in the store. After enjoying the festivities on the circle in "the Springs," Myrna and I, along with our longtime friends, Maria and Professor Lloyd Mitchell, stopped in at Stadnik's for some ice cream.

While sitting there, we were talking about Burdine's (and this book), and incredibly, the woman at the next table said, "I couldn't help but overhearing you talking about Burdine's and that you are writing a book about the store...I *loved* Burdine's!"

An animated discussion ensued, and her wonderful memories of so many happy times there poured out, but the conclusion of the discussion was what hit me hardest: "I work downtown and I can see the store from my office window, and the big 'Burdine's' sign always made me feel as if it—and I— belonged there. When I went to Burdine's I felt as if it was *our store*, but then Macy's came along, put up their big red star, removed the Burdine's name and put up the Macy's name, and I haven't walked into the store since, nor do I intend to. It's not my—or Miami's—store anymore."

So little remains from the transition years that show the "Burdine's-Macy's" name, but fortunately for posterity, the author preserved the envelope shown here, which was sent to him complete with the new Burdine's-Macy's credit card enclosed.

It is all gone now; nothing is left but the history and memories all too quickly fading. What was Burdine's is now Macy's, and there is no feeling at all of a hometown store but rather simply a realization that resistance, unhappily, was futile.

It is unbelievable how much Burdine's meant to Greater Miami, as well as to so much of Florida, and stories such as that one abound. Federated Stores may know how to *run* the stores, but taking away the names of the stores that meant so much to their various hometowns was like removing part of a city's heritage, and that was not, no matter what spin is put on it, the right thing to do. In any case, it has been done; Miami's, and Florida's, greatest name in retailing is now nothing but a warm recollection.

Although the name is gone, the stores, in our hearts, minds and photographs, will live on and on and on. May the memories of a once great store and its equally wonderful employees be remembered forever in the history of the "Magic City" and, indeed, in the history and memory of every place in Florida that was fortunate enough to have had a store in their community named Burdine's.

Appendix
Recipes

OUR SPECIAL SOUTHERN PECAN PIE

1 unbaked pie crust shell
¼ cup butter
1 cup brown sugar (light or dark)
3 eggs
½ cup light corn syrup
1½ cups pecans
1 teaspoon vanilla extract
1 cup heavy cream
1 teaspoon granulated sugar

1. Preheat oven to 375 degrees F.
2. Set aside pie crust shell. Do not pre-bake.
3. Cream together butter and sugar. Beat in eggs, one at a time.
4. Stir in corn syrup, pecans and vanilla.
5. Fill unbaked pie shell and bake 40 minutes. Let cool.
6. Whip cream with sugar. Serve pie with whipped cream and/or vanilla ice cream. Serves 6.

Following is the recipe for Burdine's very popular (and cooling) salad, which was served in the Miami store and is shown on the Tropical Tearoom menu dated February 14, 1949.

SUNSHINE FRUIT PLATE

(Individual serving)

Place lettuce leaf on bottom of a tea plate on which a papaya ring will be placed. Arrange cottage cheese in center of plate molded in egg cup, with a maraschino cherry on top of cheese. Place sections of grapefruit, orange, sliced banana and pineapple around cottage cheese mold, alternating each fruit in turn until plate is filled with a goodly portion. Serve with side of cream cheese and tropical marmalade along with a sauce boat of guest's choice of dressing, which is placed on a five-inch plate covered with a doily. Crisp saltine crackers should be placed on the dressing plate. Guest may subsitute Ry-krisp if desired.

BREAD

BURDINE'S BACON BISCUITS

2 strips bacon
2 cups of ground cornmeal
1 teaspoon salt
1 teaspoon baking soda
2 cups buttermilk
2 eggs
3 to 4 tablespoons mayonnaise

Heat oven to 450 degrees. Place 2 strips of bacon, cut into small pieces, in iron skillet in oven. Brown bacon while mixing remaining ingredients. Pour off bacon drippings and then pour cornmeal mixture on top of crisp bacon pieces in very hot skillet. Cook about 35 to 45 minutes. Serves 8.

QUICKBREAD

MARGO'S CHEESE BREAD

$3^1/_3$ cups baking mix, such as Bisquick
$1^1/_4$ cups milk
2 eggs, beaten
1 teaspoon dill weed
8 ounces sharp cheddar cheese, shredded

Combine all ingredients until mixed and pour into eight-inch loaf pan. Bake at 350 degrees for 55 minutes, until golden and baked through. Serves 10.

About the Author

S eth Bramson is Miami's foremost and premier historian. He is America's single most-published Florida history book author, with sixteen of his twenty-one books dealing directly with the villages, towns, cities, counties, people and businesses of the South Florida Gold Coast.

He is the company historian of the Florida East Coast Railway—one of only two people in the country who bears that title with an American railroad—and his book *Speedway to Sunshine* is the official history of that famous line. His collection of FEC Railway and Florida transportation memorabilia is the largest in the world; it is larger than the state museum's collection and larger than the Flagler Museum's collection.

A graduate of Cornell University's famed School of Hotel Administration, he holds master's degrees from St. Thomas University and Florida International University, both located in Miami. He is adjunct professor of history and historian in residence at Barry University and adjunct professor of history at Florida International University, where he teaches all of the university's South

Florida and Florida history courses. In addition he is historian in residence at FIU's Osher Lifelong Learning Institute.

The founder of the Miami Memorabilia Collectors Club, his collection of Miami memorabilia and Floridiana is the largest in private hands in the country.

He is now working on his twenty-second and twenty-third books, the tentative titles of which are *Jewels in the Sunshine: The Flagler System Hotels* and *Beach is Dynamite!: The History of Miami Beach High.*

Additionally, he is the author of more than 110 articles on South Florida local and Florida transportation history, including four in juried or refereed publications.

He has appeared as a featured guest or commentator on Florida history programs on A&E, Discovery Channel, Florida Public Broadcasting, FX's *The Collectibles Show*, History Channel, Learning Channel and Turner South Network, as well as all five local Miami television stations.

Nationally recognized as Florida's leading transportation historian and the Miami area's preeminent local historian, he has been quoted frequently in newspapers and magazines throughout Florida, as well as in the *New York Times*, the *Chicago Tribune*, *Bloomberg Business Week*, *History*, the *History Channel Magazine* and *USA Today*.